NATURE
OF
SNOWDONIA

A BEGINNER'S GUIDE TO THE UPLAND ENVIRONMENT

MIKE RAINE

Cover photos include: feral goat by Morag McGrath and Snowdon by Pierino Algieri.

First published in Great Britain 2010 by Pesda Press
Unit 22, Galeri
Doc Victoria
Caernarfon
Gwynedd
LL55 1SQ

© Copyright 2010 Mike Raine

ISBN: 978-1-906095-10-9

Printed in Poland, produced by Polska Book.

CONTENTS

ACKNOWLEDGEMENTS

I'm very lucky to have been closely associated with Dr Janet Summer for many years. Janet has done a splendid job of providing us with an accessible and practical introduction to the geology of Snowdonia as well as commenting and contributing to many other aspects of this book. Without her contribution, it would have been a lesser work. I am also extremely grateful to Brian Green and Dr Barbara Jones who checked my lichen and fungus, and flower, fern and moss identifications, respectively. Thanks also to Elfyn Jones for input on the farming and land-use section and to Keith Ball for the photographs of the rose chafer and the golden ringed dragonfly, Carlo Forte for the Snowdon lily shot and Ange Boysen for the adder. Finally, I would like to thank the students and staff of Plas y Brenin for encouragement and inspiration, as well as putting up with me dropping to my knees or disappearing into the undergrowth to photograph some previously unnoticed specimen.

INTRODUCTION

Walking and climbing amongst these hills, it will not be long before you start to wonder about that strange flower or that high-pitched bird call, how the rocks came to be so varied or why the landscape is so dramatic. How do you find these things out? I have been frustrated by wading through copious field guides to lichens, mosses, birds, flowers and rocks to discover more about the things we see around us. I asked myself, what is that pretty yellow flower I see everywhere? What bird sang that strange high-pitched song? Why does the rock seem so very different on every hillside?

The aim of this small book is to bring together information into one handy guide to help you learn about and appreciate the places we walk and climb. It's a beginner's guide to the four seasons of our small but delightful mountains. I have tried to distil it down to the most common things you will see out and about in the hills of Snowdonia. I can only apologise if I have missed out something you find.

The four sections to this guide are; winter, spring, summer and autumn. There are of course some things you can see all year round. However, while distracted by the beautiful array of wild flowers in the summer you may be forgiven for overlooking your geology. That said, winter is the perfect time for studying rocks and lichens.

I hope that most people know their daisies from their daffodils and their daffodils from their dandelions. But there are many common plants that simply pass unnoticed as we continue on our mountain adventures. I hope a little knowledge of the tormentil, thyme and thrift will enhance your day in the mountains. I have avoided the obscure in favour of the obvious, but I have included a note on a handful of Snowdonia's iconic rarities. I have struggled to identify esoteric mosses, lichens and fungi, so please forgive me if I have overlooked more than I have included.

Alongside many of the species I have noted their culinary and medicinal uses. Most of these are what you might call 'traditional', none have been tested by me, and none are recommended for experimentation. I include them merely as points of interest to help remember the species. It is considered bad form to pick wild flowers, indeed many are protected by law. Take only photographs and leave things as they are for other people to enjoy.

The bibliography should be considered one of the most important aspects of this book and I hope that you will be inspired to learn more about the wildlife of Snowdonia.

Happy walking and climbing!

Mike Raine

Warning

Leave the plants and animals you discover as you find them. Do not pick plants and do not eat them. Traditional medicinal uses mentioned in this book are for interest only.

Proper names

Throughout, I have used the common names of things. Alongside these names you may often read the scientific Latin name in *green* or the Welsh name in **red**.

Brachiopod fossils on Y Garn above
Cwm Clyd, a reminder of the
impermanence and astonishing diversity
of life everywhere around us.

WINTER

Snowdon or Yr Wyddfa.

Looking down into Twll Du, commonly known as The Devil's Kitchen, in Cwm Idwal.

ROCK & ICE

by Dr Janet Summer

From across Llynnau Mymbyr, the view of Snowdon is instantly recognisable, the iconic image of the symbol of North Wales. At the risk of stating the obvious, it is made of rock. Beyond that not many people will have given it further consideration. Most of us never really look at the rocks around us, other than to make an assessment of how difficult a level of climbing or scrambling they might represent. Just a little geological knowledge will allow some of the many wonderful mysteries of our planet's history, and particularly our mountain environments, to be unravelled. Rocks are remarkable in that they have travelled greatly in both space and time, from warm Bahamian waters to huge volcanoes spewing ash to lava erupting underwater 600 million years ago. Most of the earth's major processes such as volcanic eruptions, mountain building, weathering, erosion and earthquakes involve rocks and minerals; every rock contains clues about the environment in which it was formed.

In order to spot these clues to unravel the mysteries and appreciate both the 'hard' landscape as well as the wildlife that exists upon it, here's a brief guide to geology in general and a look at the rocks of Snowdonia in particular.

Common rock types

There is a finite amount of mineral matter forming our planet, so the rocks of the earth are constantly being recycled and transformed into new types of rock by a number of processes which together comprise the rock cycle. There are three basic rock types in this cycle: igneous, sedimentary and metamorphic. Each of these rock types can be distinguished by recognising the size, shape and arrangement of the mineral grains from which they are made.

Igneous rocks

Igneous rocks are considered as the start of the rock cycle – how a rock is 'born'. All igneous rocks have solidified from molten rock called magma, either inside the earth or on its surface. The extrusion of magma onto the earth's surface by volcanoes produces lava and hot fragments. These are called pyroclasts; 'pyro' and 'clast' stem from the Greek words for fire and fragment, respectively. Examples of pyroclasts include pumice and ash. These types of rocks are called extrusive igneous rocks. Other igneous rocks, such as granite, form deep underground and are called intrusive igneous rocks as the magma has cooled and solidified within the earth.

Magma is a complex chemical soup, containing many elements that organise themselves into certain minerals as the magma cools and begins to crystallise. Different sorts of mineral in an igneous rock begin to crystallise at different temperatures, but the fundamental control on the mineral composition of an igneous rock is the chemistry of the magma from which it crystallises. However, chemistry is not the only thing that makes igneous rocks look different.

Molten rock erupting.
© iStockphoto.com

Some igneous rocks can have exactly the same chemical composition, but appear different because of the size of the crystals. The number and size of the crystals depends on the amount of time they had to grow. In extrusive rocks, this can be from seconds (imagine a small fragment of magma flying through the air) to a few years (for the middle of a thick lava flow e.g. basalt). This kind of rapid cooling results in small crystals because they have had very little time to grow. For intrusive igneous rocks, the cooling time is much slower (several thousand years) so there is time for much larger crystals to grow. Generally speaking, the slower the cooling the bigger are the crystals.

Columnar joints

Columnar joints are a feature of igneous rocks. They are most common in basalt lava flows, classic examples being the Giant's Causeway in Northern Ireland and Fingal's Cave in the Inner Hebrides. However, they also occur in extrusive volcanic rocks of rhyolitic composition (such as in Snowdonia). They form during the cooling and crystallisation of molten rock. Perfect columns are hexagonal in cross section and interlocking.

The hexagonal shape is the most efficient way of losing the thermal energy released during the rapid cooling and crystallisation of the rock. The cooling cracks start to grow from the top and base of the flow where the cooling is most rapid, and then propagate down into the flow forming columns.

Perfect interlocking hexagonal columnar joints, formed during the cooling of molten volcanic rock.

Columnar joints near Llyn Teyrn.

Sedimentary rocks

Sedimentary rocks can be considered 'new rocks' formed by the geological processes acting on existing rocks. Sedimentary rocks form under a great variety of circumstances from glaciers to deserts, rivers and coral reefs. They are formed by the settling out (deposition) of tiny grains which form layers or beds of sediment.

Bedded gritstone on the Lleyn Peninsular. The horizontal breaks are bedding planes, highlighting how the sediment was deposited in layers, and are a good indicator of a sedimentary rock.

Grains of sediment are made by the weathering of exposed rock, broken up by water, wind, frost and ice. The tiny fragments and individual mineral grains are usually transported from one place to another by wind, water or flowing ice before being deposited somewhere calmer as roughly horizontal layers of sediment.

These layers of sediment may themselves become washed or blown away, but if they survive they may become buried by yet more sediment. The weight of overlying sediment compacts the older sediment below. This tends to squeeze out any water, especially if new minerals grow in the spaces between the grains. Eventually, the loose sediment grains become cemented together forming a solid sedimentary rock such as sandstone. Because sediments are laid down in layers, these 'beds' or layers are often seen preserved in the rock – a good indication of sedimentary origin.

An example of another classic and well-known sedimentary rock, limestone, taken at Pen Trwyn on the Great Orme. Limestone comprises many of the UK's (and Europe's) premier climbing and scrambling destinations.

Completely new sedimentary rocks can form by biological processes such as the accumulation of shells or the growth of coral reefs. Corals and shells are principally formed of the mineral calcite. When calcite accumulates in great thicknesses, it forms limestone.

An expanse of banded and folded metamorphic rock, Red Wall, Gogarth on Anglesey. Under pressure and/or reheating, metamorphic rocks have usually re-crystallised. They are often very hard but also brittle, making for entertaining climbing!

Exotically coloured, marbled, banded and fragmented metamorphic rock on Llanddwyn Island, Anglesey.

Metamorphic rocks

Metamorphic rocks are existing sedimentary and igneous rocks that have been changed in form. Any type of rock can become a metamorphic rock; it simply requires heating to temperatures of several hundred degrees Celsius and/or high pressure. An increase in pressure and temperature will occur if a rock becomes more deeply buried in the earth's surface as a result of an ever-thickening cover of sedimentary deposits, or as a result of earth movements. This often happens at the boundaries of the earth's tectonic plates where, for example, two continents may collide forming new mountain ranges. Under very extreme conditions, deeply buried metamorphic rocks can begin to melt and produce new magma. Igneous and metamorphic rocks both have a crystalline texture and are formed at high temperatures. However, metamorphism occurs in the solid state whereas igneous rocks form from liquid (molten) rock.

During metamorphism, the atoms in the minerals that make up the rock reorganise themselves into new minerals that are more suited to the new temperature and pressure conditions. As a result, the new rock may look very different from the original rock; For example, re-crystallisation can often result in banding or alignment of crystals in the rock. Overall however the chemical composition of the rock usually remains the same.

It is correct to assume that metamorphic rocks are more complex than igneous and sedimentary rocks. In general, they are more difficult to identify and interpret. Two well-known metamorphic rocks are slate and marble. However the colloquial use of the terms 'slate' and 'marble' covers a much wider range of materials than the strict metamorphic definitions.

Slate is a metamorphic rock with an extremely fine grain size; it is difficult to determine individual crystals even with a hand lens. It was originally laid down as a soft mud or silt and has been heated under pressure and re-crystallised. The result is a hard, water-resistant rock that can be split into thin sheets (completely unrelated to the original sedimentary layering), which makes it an ideal rock for roofing tiles. For more on slate, see the end of the chapter.

Marble is a metamorphic rock formed from limestone but, unlike slate, marble doesn't have a banded or flaky structure. This is because marble contains only one mineral, calcite, so there cannot be alternating bands of different minerals. This means that marble doesn't break along preferred directions like slate, making it the preferred choice of rock for sculptors. Impurities in the rock such as iron give it the coloured marbled effect.

Slate (metamorphosed mudstone) exposed in the Llanberis slate quarries, a favourite haunt for climbers. High-quality slate was removed for roofing tiles and the remainder piled into spoil heaps, a familiar site around Snowdonia.

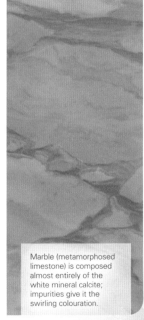

Marble (metamorphosed limestone) is composed almost entirely of the white mineral calcite; impurities give it the swirling colouration.

Iron pyrites.

Iron pyrites

It is true that there is gold in the Welsh mountains, but you are unlikely to come across it. You are more likely to see and become excited about the mineral iron pyrites, otherwise known as 'fool's gold'. Its name is derived from that fact that many miners did mistake it for the real thing. Sadly, it is practically worthless, although pristine examples will fetch money in gem shops.

Iron pyrites is a form of iron ore (iron sulphide) and is usually found in its crystal form, which is small, cubic crystals in quartz veins.

What rock is it?

So how might you distinguish between these three basic rock types? The following will probably make any geologists howl with dismay; however, this is a beginner's guide and is by no means comprehensive.

When classifying a rock the first question to ask is: **Has it got grains or crystals?** This will determine if it is sedimentary rock.

Grains are usually rounded because the minerals have been rolled around

A close-up of sandstone, revealing rounded grains.

Granite, showing interlocking angular crystals.

and transported in some way. Sand-sized grains are unsurprisingly indicative of sandstones, usually suggesting a river bed, estuary or beach. Red sandstones are very typical of deserts and are rarely formed anywhere else (the red colour is iron oxide coating the grains). Larger grains, gravel and pebbles are found in rocks such as millstone grit and conglomerates (a collection of pebbles and fine silt) and indicate more energetic environments such as river deltas and flash floods.

Crystals are typically angular, interlocking and often reflect light off their surfaces giving the rock a sparkly look. Ask yourself another question: **If the rock has crystals, are they large or small?** Remember large crystals mean slow cooling at depth (intrusive igneous e.g. granite) and small crystals mean much more rapid cooling such as basalt lava flows (extrusive igneous). Finally: **Is there evidence of banding and folding in the rock?** This may suggest the rock is metamorphic rather than igneous.

An example of intensely folded ash fall tuff at the base of Clogwyn Du'r Arddu; the pattern of the fold is highlighted by the thin layers of ash.

Folding

To most of us rock is hard, brittle stuff. However, over extremely long periods of (geological) time, they can be bent and folded without fracturing, in a plastic manner. Folding occurs when the rock is compressed, such as when tectonic plates collide.

Folding can occur on grand scales visible across cliff faces (see later, the Idwal syncline); indeed, whole mountain ranges can result from folding. However it can also be seen in pebble-sized rock samples and even at the microscopic scale. Folds are most easily seen in well-bedded sedimentary rocks, where the bedding planes trace out the pattern of the fold.

Examples of fossils in sedimentary rocks; (left) a fossil trilobite in shale, found on Pen yr Ole Wen and (right) fossil shells in limestone.

You'll soon realise that fine-grained rocks are a bit of a headache. This is because they are too fine to determine if the grains are actually grains or crystals. Some background knowledge of the area can be useful.

Broadly speaking, fine-grained rocks are formed in two ways. They can be laid down in very low-energy environments such as the bottom of the ocean, lakes or in large estuaries (where rivers enter the sea and their silt finally settles out). The process is very slow and it can take thousands of years for the deposit to accumulate. The presence of fossils (fragments of shells and corals are most common) is a dead giveaway of a sedimentary rock. Fossils are usually found in limestone, chalk and sometimes shale.

Alternatively, an explosive volcanic eruption can produce a vast amount of fine-grained ash almost instantaneously, usually deposited on the exposed flanks of volcanoes. When the volcano is close to the sea or a lake, however, the ash has to settle through the water column in the same manner as silt or mud. This leads to the argument of whether it is igneous or sedimentary. It is, however, still regarded as an igneous rock because of its volcanic origin.

It will be apparent by now that rock identification is every bit as challenging and interesting as identifying birds, flowers and ferns, but definitely easier than identifying lichens and fungi!

Rock quiz

~⅓rd scale

Try this quiz and see if you can identify any of the rocks. You might improve your score after reading through the rest of this section (answers on page 34). You can also try analysing rock samples online at: open2.net/sciencetechnologynature/worldaroundus/toolkit/whatrock.html

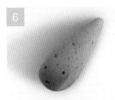

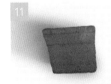

An artist's impression of Cwm Idwal. The different layers of rock have been highlighted in colour. © Anthony Cane

Setting the scene

Cwm Idwal in the Ogwen Valley is an excellent place to become familiar with the rocks and geological history of Snowdonia. Most of the rock types typical to Snowdonia can be seen while walking around Cwm Idwal. The same rocks are also encountered in the Llanberis Pass, around Capel Curig and on Snowdon itself.

There is no getting away from the fact that the geology of Snowdonia is extremely complex. Firstly, the rocks are very old. They were formed between 495 and 443 million years ago (during the Ordovician period) and have been subject to rather a beating since then. Secondly, although most of the rocks are from volcanoes that were active at that time, there was

Large-scale folding, the 'syncline' (the upward-curving concave shape) at the back of Cwm Idwal.

also a sea nearby which made its own sedimentary deposits, into which some of the volcanic products became mixed. Added to this a tectonic collision forced up a mountain range as high as the Alps, which has subsequently eroded to the mountains we see now.

I make no apologies for glossing over some (indeed most) of the detail, in order to make my account of the geological history of Snowdonia easy to remember. It is intended to provide a few mental images to take into the mountains with you.

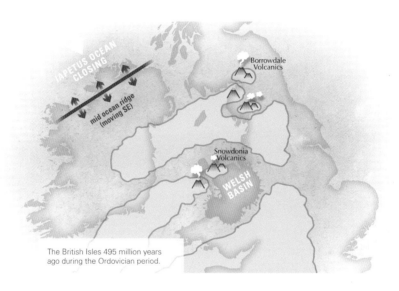

The British Isles 495 million years ago during the Ordovician period.

About 495 million years ago, the British Isles looked nothing like they do today. There was a landmass to the south called Avalonia, which is approximately southern England today. Wales was a shallow sea known as the Welsh Basin, there was another small landmass roughly where Ireland is today and beyond that was an ocean known as the Iapetus Ocean. On the other side of the Iapetus, a landmass known as Laurentia (now Scotland) was heading inexorably towards us, driven by the movement of the plates and bulldozing everything in its path. As Scotland advanced, the Iapetus Ocean slowly closed due to subduction or being forced down and under the plates hosting the landmasses of Scotland and England.

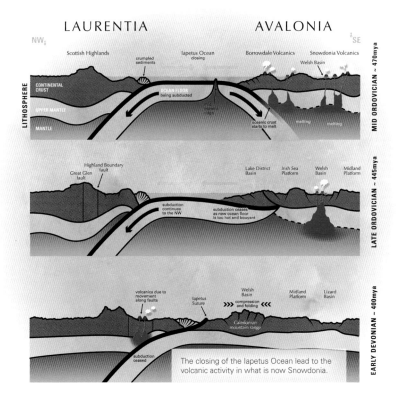

LAURENTIA

AVALONIA

The closing of the Iapetus Ocean lead to the volcanic activity in what is now Snowdonia.

Typically, when plates are forced down deep into and below the earth's crust, they melt producing molten rock that eventually find its way up towards the surface to erupt as volcanoes or to be intruded at depth in the form of granite and similar rocks. In the Welsh Basin significant volumes of volcanic material were erupted, forming a series of volcanic islands surrounded by shallow seas (quite a different picture from today!)

Eventually the Iapetus Ocean closed and the two land masses collided, crumpling and folding the Welsh volcanoes and the sea-floor sediments between them and thrusting the land up into a huge chain of mountains known as the Caledonian Mountains. These mountains, which were once as high as the Alps, have been eroded to stumps by the action of water and, more recently, the ice age. The landscape of Snowdonia has a tortuous history.

This condensed history lays out the setting for the formation of the rocks in Snowdonia, but will not really help with identification. For that, a crash-course in volcanology is also needed. Sadly, extrusive igneous rocks are not as simple as just basalt lava flows and ash. Explosive volcanoes produce a huge variety of deposits, which vary according to just how explosive the volcano is, the chemistry of the magma and the distance from the volcano (windblown ash can travel much further than a lava flow).

A quick guide to volcanic rocks

Molten rock (magma) can erupt quietly and effusively, flowing out over the surface as lava flows, or it can erupt violently and explosively when escaping gas tears the magma into tiny fragments called pyroclasts. Pyroclasts come in all shapes and sizes from minute ash particles to volcanic 'bombs' many metres in diameter. The explosive nature of a volcano is largely governed by the chemical composition of the magma.

There are two compositions for magma: [1] acidic (felsic) magmas which crystallise (solidify) to form mainly pale minerals such as feldspar and quartz. [2] basic (mafic) magmas which contain more iron and magnesium and crystallise to produce dark minerals and less feldspar and quartz.

Rhyolite, a fine-grained extrusive volcanic rock. It is acidic in composition, comprised mostly pale minerals and weathers to a characteristic creamy-buff colour. Rhyolites are often associated with explosive volcanic eruptions.

Basalt, a fine-grained extrusive volcanic rock. It is basic in composition, comprises mainly dark minerals and is typically dark grey to black in colour. Basalts are often associated with quiescent volcanic eruptions.

Acidic magmas tend to be thick and viscous and erupt explosively; basic magmas tend to be runnier and often erupt more quietly. The chemical composition of magma not only effects on how it erupts, but also the colour of the resultant rocks.

Acidic rocks contain lots of pale minerals such as quartz and feldspar, so they tend to be pale in colour. Since they usually contain some iron they often weather to a characteristic buff or pinkish-brown colour. Magma erupted in violent, explosive eruptions is usually rhyolitic magma.

Basic rocks contain lots of dark minerals, so they are typically dark in colour. The composition of magma erupted in effusive, gentle lava flow eruptions is most often basaltic.

Quartz veins and nodules

Brilliant-white veins of quartz are a common sight around Snowdonia. Quartz is a mineral made of silica; it is quite hard and will scratch a knife blade or pane of glass. It commonly occurs in veins and nodules.

As rocks fracture under intense folding or due to the intrusion of magma, fluidal quartz will shoot along the cracks and crystallise, forming long narrow veins. Quartz-rich fluids can also find their way through sediments and porous volcanic deposits like ash fall and ash flows. The quartz may start to crystallise around a fossil or volcanic fragment to form a quartz nodule.

A quartz vein at Cwm Bochlwyd. Closer inspection will reveal the prismatic quartz crystals making up the vein.

Quartz nodules on Tryfan, crystallised out of solution, around hard fragments.

Classifying rocks may seem relatively simple so far, but there is a sting in the tail: the size of the crystals can also influence the colour of a rock. Because of the way crystals reflect light, rocks comprising minute crystals can look much darker than their chemical composition would suggest (volcanic glass is usually black whatever its composition). So take a look both at both fresh and weathered surfaces. Fresh surfaces are good for seeing the crystals and texture in the rock, while the weathered surfaces might offer more clues to the chemical composition.

The rocks in Snowdonia are mainly extrusive, rhyolitic volcanics, the majority of which are the result of explosive eruptions. The rocks are known as the Snowdon Volcanic Group (see the *Geological Special Sheet to Central Snowdonia*, 1:25 000, produced by the British Geological Survey). There is an occasional basalt lava flow in the mix, some sediments such as sandstone and, of course, the ubiquitous slate (metamorphosed mudstone).

Products of explosive eruptions

It is easy to discern the sandstone and slate, but volcanic eruptions produce a variety of related rock types, depending on the circumstances.

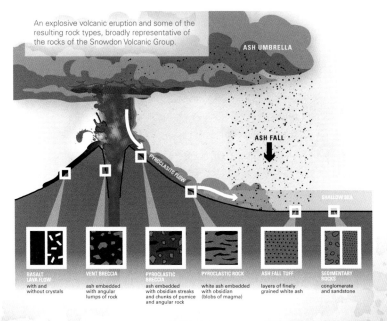

An explosive volcanic eruption and some of the resulting rock types, broadly representative of the rocks of the Snowdon Volcanic Group.

ASH UMBRELLA

ASH FALL

PYROCLASTIC FLOW

SHALLOW SEA

BASALT LAVA FLOW with and without crystals

VENT BRECCIA ash embedded with angular lumps of rock

PYROCLASTIC BRECCIA ash embedded with obsidian streaks and chunks of pumice and angular rock

PYROCLASTIC ROCK white ash embedded with obsidian (blobs of magma)

ASH FALL TUFF layers of finely grained white ash

SEDIMENTARY ROCKS conglomerate and sandstone

Molten rock squeezes upwards through weaknesses in the earth's crust and may eventually erupt out of the vent of a volcano. Magma typically contains a lot of dissolved gases such as carbon dioxide and steam. As the pressure on the magma is released, the gases come out of solution to form bubbles. The expansion of these bubbles and the speed at which the magma is forced out of the vent causes the molten rock to be ripped into innumerable tiny fragments or pyroclasts. A good analogy is to shake a bottle of fizzy drink and then take the top off!

Layers of thinly bedded, fine-grained ash fall tuff in Cwm Idwal.

The gas and pyroclasts are ejected out of the vent and form a huge umbrella-shaped cloud laden with ash and fragments. The cloud spreads out and fine ash begins to rain down. When the ash settles it forms a 'pyroclastic fall deposit', also known as an 'ash **fall** tuff' which blankets the flanks and the ground downwind of the volcano. Ash can also fall into the sea and subsequently settle to the ocean floor. Whether it settles through water or air, falling ash is deposited like a sediment and is usually laid down in thin layers or beds. The minute grain size and multiple thin layers are characteristic of ash fall, and are the main things to look for when out on the hill. It also often weathers to a pale creamy-white colour.

Tuff is a consolidated rock composed of pyroclastic fragments and fine ash. If the particles are still hot when they land and then stick or weld together, it is called a '**welded** tuff'.

Tuff can form in two ways: by ash falling to the ground (as described above) or by ash flowing. If the umbrella cloud becomes too heavily laden with ash and pyroclasts, gravity kicks in and parts of it collapse forming smaller, very dense, clouds which roll down the sides of the volcano rather like a landslide. In this case, the particles are carried along by hot air and gases from the volcano instead of water. When these dense pyroclastic flows loose their momentum they deposit their load forming a pyroclastic flow deposit or 'ash **flow** tuff'.

Two examples of The Pits Head Tuff (left and right), a welded ash flow deposit. Often referred to as 'zebra-striped rock'.

Deposition usually happens quite quickly, and can result in a massive layer up to several metres thick. Ash flow deposits lack the fine layers of ash fall deposits. Because these clouds are very dense, they often carry lots of larger fragments as well as ash and if the particles are still hot, the deposit will stick together forming a welded ash flow tuff (sometimes called an ignimbrite). Molten particles become squashed when this happens, so the rock may end up with streaky, glassy fragments in it.

Many of the rocks in the Snowdonia area are ash flow tuffs, and some are more welded than others. A classic example of a welded ash flow tuff in Snowdonia is the 'Pitts Head Tuff'; a striking-looking rock that is very obvious in the field and was used as a marker horizon when the geology of the area was mapped. It weathers black and white rather like zebra stripes. The white fine-grained material is ash and the darker fragments are the once-molten bits of rock that have been squashed into flattened glassy streaks. Pieces of Pits Head Tuff can be seen in the path leading up to Cwm Idwal. Once identified, it can be seen quite frequently.

There is one more volcanic rock type which would be useful to recognise. It is particularly obvious up at the back of Cwm Idwal around the Devil's Kitchen. It is a coarse-grained and poorly sorted rock, meaning it comprises lots of fragments of different sizes surrounded by fine ash. It is volcanic breccia (breccia is the term used to describe a rock made up of broken fragments). There are many types of breccia, but we will only deal with the volcanic kind.

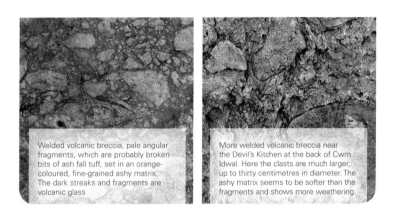

Welded volcanic breccia, pale angular fragments, which are probably broken bits of ash fall tuff, set in an orange-coloured, fine-grained ashy matrix. The dark streaks and fragments are volcanic glass

More welded volcanic breccia near the Devil's Kitchen at the back of Cwm Idwal. Here the clasts are much larger, up to thirty centimetres in diameter. The ashy matrix seems to be softer than the fragments and shows more weathering.

Differential weathering

Walking around the mountains as a novice geologist one can see all kinds of interesting and inexplicable structures in the rocks that warrant a second look – don't try to identify everything. The photograph above right is a good example, prompting wild speculation about the formation of these bowl-like features. They are in fact just the result of differential weathering. It may be where a quartz nodule has fallen out of the rock or could simply be a part of the rock that is not as strongly welded or cemented together as the rest. Many unusual features and colours are the result of weathering.

In a volcanic breccia, the fragments are usually bits of the rock that make up the volcano; fragments of lava flows, chunks of ash fall deposits and bits of pyroclastic flow deposits, from centimetres to meters across. Geologically speaking, volcanoes grow quite fast and as a result they can be unstable. Parts of the flanks frequently collapse and come tumbling down rather like landslides. When they come to rest, the jumbled mass consolidates into a rock comprising great quantities of different fragments, ash and sometimes also molten material. These are sometimes called pyroclastic breccias.

Volcanic breccias can also form around the vent of a volcano during explosive eruptions. Vent breccia results from the vent being blown to bits when fragments are thrown out and fall back around the vent. Again, if there are any hot particles the whole deposit can weld together.

If in doubt about the precise origin of a breccia, then simply refer to it as volcanic breccia.

The fragments in a breccia are usually angular because they have not undergone prolonged transport by water which would round them into cobbles. Rocks containing rounded fragments are usually laid down by rivers of flash floods and are called conglomerates.

Although this is a simplified guide to rock identification, it is a useful one. If you're a complete beginner in geological classification, try the walk around Cwm Idwal as a starting point in order to identify the volcanic rocks. Remember that the different rock types can occur in layers, one on top of the other, and that they may be inter-layered with sediments such as sandstones and mudstones. You will soon be able to pick out these rock types on scrambles around Snowdonia.

If this whistle-stop tour of the rocks of Snowdonia has sparked off a real interest in geology, try *Teach Yourself Geology* by David Rothery. For a more thorough knowledge of the geology of Snowdonia, *Rock Trails Snowdonia* by Paul Gannon is thoroughly recommended. It documents a number of walks in Snowdonia and provides detailed descriptions and explanations of the geological features encountered on the way.

Rock quiz answers ↺

1 Ash flow tuff – The black flame-shaped streaks of volcanic glass indicate that this rock comprises once-molten fragments. These fragments are set in very fine-grained white volcanic ash. The rock is poorly sorted, bits too large and very tiny fragments, suggesting that it is likely to be the deposit of an ash flow rather than an ash fall. The very pale colour of the ash suggests a rhyolitic composition. The flattened nature of the black glassy fragments suggests this is a welded ash flow tuff. The rock is, in fact, a sample of the Pitts Head Tuff.

2 Desert sandstone – Layered and comprised of sand-sized grains that make it a sandstone. The red coloration (which is an oxidised iron coating on the grains) indicates it was laid down in an arid, desert environment.

3 Conglomerate pebble – The rounding of this rock is due to the action of water; rounding can either obscure or enhance the texture of a rock. In this case, sub-angular fragments of pale-coloured rock are clearly visible in a fine-grained red matrix. This rock is poorly sorted with both large and fine fragments. Poorly sorted rocks are often the result of rapid deposition (with little chance for water or wind to sort out the grain sizes). The red coloration suggests an arid environment. This conglomerate is probably the result of a flash flood in a desert.

4 Granite – Interlocking crystals which vary in size and colour. The large crystal size and predominance of pale minerals indicate that this rock is granite.

5 Ash fall tuff – This rock has an extremely small grain size and faint layering. It appears dark grey on freshly cut surfaces, but weathers to a creamy-buff colour which is typical of rhyolite compositions. The colour, fine grain size and layering suggest that this is an ash fall tuff of rhyolite composition (as opposed to a mudstone or slate which are dark on both weathered and fresh surfaces).

6 Pumice – A volcanic rock, often found lurking in the bathroom. It's rough, full of holes and light in the hand. The holes represent once-trapped bubbles of gas. Pumice is produced by frothing of magma during an eruption (as trapped gas tries to expand and escape). The pale colour indicates a rhyolitic composition.

7 Volcanic glass (obsidian) – This rock has no grains at all. Once-molten rock that has chilled or vitrified (turned to glass) almost instantaneously at eruption. This rapid chilling does not allow time for crystals to grow. The dark colour of the glass is due to impurities such as iron and magnesium.

8 Porphyritic granite – Interlocking crystals, variable in size and colour. More than half the crystals are pale in colour which, together with the large crystal size, indicate the rock is a granite. There are some obvious large pink crystals. Such large crystals are known as phenocrysts; they start growing very early within the magma chamber and can reach very large sizes. Rocks containing such large phenocrysts are prefixed by the word 'porphyritic'.

9 Quartz pebble – This rounded water-worn pebble is not a rock at all. It is made entirely of crystals of a single mineral: quartz.

10 Granite pebble – This pebble is water washed, and a good example of how weathering can make rocks more difficult to identify. The crystalline texture is less obvious here than in fresh samples such as 4 and 8.

11 Lacustrine sandstone – Consisting entirely of layers of fine sand-sized grains. The yellowish-grey colour is typical of sandstones laid down in lakes (lacustrine), rivers and beach environments. The dark bands could represent bits of trapped organic matter like leaves and fragments of bark.

12 Quartz crystal – This is an example of quartz in its purest, crystalline form.

13 Basalt – This dark, finely crystalline rock is basalt. It is made up predominantly of dark minerals. The small crystal size is due to the molten rock cooling very quickly as it was extruded onto the surface. Basalt typically forms lava flows.

14 Limestone – Made up of the mineral calcite. It most obviously contains fossil fragments, in this case shells, bits of coral and fragments of a marine animal known as a crinoid or 'sea lily' (these fragments themselves are also calcite which has replaced the skeletal or hard parts of the animals). Apart from fossil fragments, limestone also contains fine material such as calcite-rich mud/silt and sometimes calcite crystals. Calcite crystals can be confusing as they give the rock a glittery, crystalline look (leading to a misidentification as an igneous rock). Look out for tiny fossil fragments to determine if it is a limestone.

15 Breccia pebble – This rounded water-worn pebble is a breccia. Notice how the fragments are consistently more angular than those in sample 3. Breccias can be formed as a result of landslides and explosive volcanic eruptions, and by intense folding and faulting which can fracture the rock in situ.

16 Siltstone – Pale grey, very fine-grained rock. Although you cannot tell from a photograph, in the field such rocks are often rather soft, crumbly and friable. Siltstone could be confused with mudstone (which is even finer grained) but a sure-fire test is to crumble a piece between finger and thumb. If it feels gritty it is a siltstone and not a mudstone. Siltstones are often finely layered or laminated.

Post-glacial landscape around Clogwyn y Person and Crib Goch.

Glaciation by Mike Raine

Although the mountains of Snowdonia once attained a height of 7,000m, today they climax at 1,000m. This is a result of 400 million years of erosion, principally by water. It may seem incredible that 6,000m of rock have been worn down to give us the landscape we so enjoy today. Ice has shaped the surface we see in a very characteristic manner. However, the role of ice in the formation of these mountains must not be overstated; its duration a mere blink of the eye in geological time.

There really isn't such a thing as the Ice Age. Ice came and went from these mountains in a series of advances and retreats. There have been many glacial and interglacial periods during the last two and a half million years. The evidence of the action of ice we see today is mainly from the last accumulation of ice during the Younger Dryas period (12,000 to 10,000 years ago). Look out for the effects of glaciation on small and large scale.

Arêtes

The steep cliffs at the back of the combe *(cwm)*, the headwall, migrate back into ridges creating the sharp arêtes we see today. A classic example is the ridge of Crib Goch.

Snow is collected in the high valleys on the mountain sides and gradually turned to ice through a process called nivation. This is most apparent on the north and east sides of the mountains, the coldest faces. This build up of ice is at odds with gravity and, in time, will slide downhill in a rotational fashion, gouging out the armchair-shaped hollows known in Snowdonia as cwms. The ice leaves a steep back wall where freeze-thaw action plucks rock from the growing cliff faces. Quite often the rotational slumping will leave a rock barrier across the mouth of a cwm, sometimes creating a lake.

Drainage pattern

Glaciers follow the path of least resistance, flowing around or over obstacles, evidence of which can be seen in the modern day drainage patterns from the cwms.

Before the Ice Age, the water from Cwm Idwal flowed eastward down what we now call the Ogwen Valley past Tryfan to Capel Curig and the Afon Llugwy. The glacier followed this route initially, but when the large glacier heading to Capel Curig from Snowdon arrived, the progress of the Ogwen Valley ice was halted. Around the area of Idwal Cottage Youth Hostel, the ice spilled over into the Nant Ffrancon. As the ice receded, the drainage from Cwm Idwal made easier progress northward down the Nant Ffrancon rather than returning to its former route past Tryfan.

Llyn Llydaw with the rock barrier clearly visible along the left-hand side of the lake.

Erratic in Cwm Clogwyn.

Blockfield created by frost shattering on top of the Glyderau.

Frost heave (left & right).

Erratics

Large irregular boulders, sometimes of distant rock types can be found perched in the strangest places. Erratics occur when large boulders carried on the moving ice, or trapped within, are dumped along the glacier's path.

Frost heave

This is one of the few freeze-thaw processes that is easy to observe in Snowdonia. Ice crystals lift up soil particles and as the ice melts, the soil particles tumble downhill. You can see soil movement of up to 5cm during a cold snap, often on the exposed soil alongside footpaths.

Frost shattering

Many of our summit landscapes are bare and rocky; this is the result of frost shattering. Frost shattering is principally a periglacial process, which means it occurred at the periphery of the ice age. Following the retreat of the ice, there would have been a long period when the temperature range during the year was much greater than it is today. This led to a massive amount of freeze-thaw weathering which formed the large scree slopes seen throughout Snowdonia as well as the blockfields in places such as the top of the Glyderau.

Pyramidal peaks – the Snowdon massif, with its many cwms and arêtes.

Scree on the south side of the Llanberis Pass. These are amongst the most stable acidic scree slopes in the world and are protected today by their SSSI designation.

Moraine below Cryn Las.

Moraines

Where glaciers stop flowing, they dump the material they have been bulldozing along leading to the formation of moraines. If the moraine is located at the end of the glacier, it is known as a terminal moraine. Lateral moraines can also occur, and are positioned alongside the glacier.

Pyramidal peaks

When walking or climbing around Snowdon, the Glyderau and the Carneddau we are in a post-glacial landscape. The large-scale features are those of cwms and arêtes. Snowdon itself is a classic pyramidal peak with deep-cut cwms on each side and sharp arêtes radiating out from its summit.

Roche moutonnée

Occasionally glaciers encounter slightly harder bands of rock beneath. These push the glacier upwards and the immense pressure leads to the melting of water at the base of the glacier. The water then flows down the other side of the obstruction and freezes on the rock, giving rise to the plucking of a steeper face. Rock formations with a smooth upstream side and a steep downstream side abound in Snowdonia, and are known by their French name of *roche moutonnée* (rock sheep).

Roche moutonnée.

Striations beside the Watkin path.

Striations

Over where the glacier flows it leaves behind scratches in the bedrock as its huge weight pushes the loose rock embedded in it down upon on the surface of the rock below. The prominence of these striations gives us an impression of the weight of ice above and is an indication of the direction in which the ice was flowing.

U-shaped valleys

During the Younger Dryas, the high valleys of Snowdonia were filled with glaciers which carved out the cwms we see today. They flowed slowly down towards the sea, widening the river valleys to form the large U-shaped valleys we see today such as the Nant Ffrancon and the Nant Gwynant. Everywhere in Snowdonia is evidence of the landscape features left behind by glaciation. U-shaped valleys often have long narrow lakes in them (ribbon lakes); these are usually quite shallow and just sit in the shallow depression left in the valley bottom by the weight of the ice. Llyn Ogwen is a good example with a maximum depth of 3m, although Llynnau Mymbyr, next to Plas y Brenin, reaches a maximum depth of 9m.

Cloud-filled Nant Ffrancon during a temperature inversion, giving the impression of a glacier-filled valley.

Nant Ffrancon, a classic U-shaped valley.

Bilberry in winter.

Foxglove without flowers.

Stonecrop without flowers.

WINTER PLANTS

Many higher plants look a bit strange in the winter. For example, Bilberry without its leaves looks nothing like the plant in summer. Here are a few plants which might confuse when seen without flowers, leaves or berries.

Bilberry *(llusen)*
Bilberry is a deciduous plant so loses its leaves in the winter. It appears as a series of simple stalks. See page 110 for bilberry in summer.

Foxglove *(bysedd y cŵn)*
The leaves of the foxglove appear long before the plant comes into flower. From February onwards, the characteristic rosette of leaves will be seen on the lower slopes of the hills well before they flower in June. The leaves of the foxgloves will be widespread during autumn after the flowers have died in September. See page 72 for flowering foxglove.

Stonecrop *(briweg y cerrig)*
The small white and pink flowers of the English stonecrop are characteristic of scree slopes and quarry spoil tips in Snowdonia. However, the flowers are only present for a couple of months in the summertime although the strange-looking succulent plants are visible all year round. See page 113 for flowering stonecrop.

Breutelia chrysocoma (and inset)

Mosses *(mwsoglau)*

Moss will be found growing in any wet patch or on damp grassland on the mountains. The bright greens of these plants can be enjoyed (especially in wet weather) all year round in the mountains. Mosses and liverworts are some of the oldest plant groups we have (with fossil records 400 million years old). They are simply-structured plants which produce spores to reproduce. These spores require water to germinate, hence mosses are usually found in damp locations.

Identification can be difficult as many species do not have common names and many look very similar. It's worth being able to identity such species as star moss *(Polytrichum commune)* and fern moss *(Hylocomium splendens)* as they are very abundant on the mountains.

Breutelia chrysocoma
This is a common moss in the mountains, growing in large furry-looking masses mixed with other species in damp areas on heath and moorland. It can be up to 10cm tall but is usually shorter in the mountains. Look out for thick brown hairs on the lower half of the stem and green hairs higher up.

Feather moss *(Thuidium tamariscinum)* **(mwsogl pluog)**
Common in damp woodlands, this pretty little moss looks like a carpet of bright-green to rich gold-brown feathers. They grow to a fairly uniform 4cm in length. It is common on damp ground around tree stumps and rocks.

Fern moss *(Hylocomium splendens)*

This very distinctive moss grows in open grasslands, heaths, moorland and woodland. It has leaves which look like little ferns, hence the common name. It has characteristic red stems about 4cm long.

Hair cap moss *(Polytrichum piliferum)*

This moss is very similar to *P. commune* (star moss). It is a little smaller and usually tucked into rocky crevices on paths. It grows to 6cm and is a slightly lighter green than *P. commune*, with silvery hair points to the leaves and occasionally bright-red rosettes can be seen on the male plants.

Polytrichum juniperinum

Similar to *P. commune* (star moss) but smaller and slightly greyish. It is recognised by the reddish-orange-tipped leaves. It is usually low-growing, but can reach heights of 7cm. In summer it has red four-sided fruit capsules. It is usually found in rockier areas than *P. commune*.

Thuidium tamariscinum.

Hylocomium splendens.

The rosettes of Polytrichum piliferum.

Polytrichum juniperium.

Sphagnum *(mwsogl y ffynhonnau)*

A walker's nightmare! There are about 200 species of sphagnum moss. Sphagnum grows in very damp acidic locations and can hold up twenty times its dry weight in water. Sphagnum is an indicator of good quality blanket bog with little artificial drainage. It is a quite vigorous coloniser and will change the ph of the area it is growing in so that other plants struggle to survive alongside it. In the UK, sphagnum moss is sought after as a liner for hanging baskets. In northern Arctic regions it is used, when dried, as an insulating material. Anaerobic acidic sphagnum bogs are known to preserve human bodies extremely well for a long time. Examples include Tollund Man and Lindow Man. Sphagnum moss has also been used for centuries as a dressing for wounds. It is absorptive and extremely acidic, inhibiting the growth of bacteria and fungi.

Star moss *(Polytrichum commune)*

This moss is very common on the hills. It grows in large clumps in most damp areas. Four-sided caps which release the spores can be seen reaching high above the plant's foliage in summer. In its mature form, its height can vary from 2cm to 40cm. People have used star moss as a decorative material all over the world. The New Zealand Maori used it to make cloaks and the leaves have also been used for brooms and brushes. It is used by some people to make a tea, which they believe dissolves kidney and gall bladder stones.

Woolly hair moss *(Racomitrium lanuginosum) (mwsogl gwlanog)*

Found on the tops of our hills and mountains often growing on and around exposed rocks. It is an early coloniser of boulder fields. It dries out in the frequent winds found at altitude and turns grey, but as soon as it gets wet it turns green immediately. It is easily recognisable from the tiny leaves which taper to a long, whitish hair point. There are some fantastic displays on some of the slate spoil tips around northern Snowdonia and on the tops of the Carneddau, where it can form distinctive heath vegetation with lichens and low-growing heather.

Sphagnum compactum (and inset)

Sphagnum capillifolium

Polytrichum commune (and left)

Racomitrium lanuginosum (and right)

Conocephalum conicum.

Pellia epiphylla.

Liverwort *(llysiau'r afu)*

These are very simple plants which always grow in wet places and can provide some much-needed greenery in the winter. Look in streams, under boulders and in other wet places. They have very thin leaves which are poorly adapted to drying out.

Conocephalum conicum
This common liverwort will be spotted growing in damp shady flushes, often sheltered by rocks. It forms flat carpets up to 20cm long. Each leaf is marked with a hexagonal pattern, where the hexagons are the plant spores. The male plant exhibits a tinge of purple near the tips of each branch.

Dripwort *(Pellia epiphylla)*
This is a common and easily-spotted liverwort which grows on damp soils. The fleshy leaves grow to 1cm across. It is often seen growing amongst the steps on footpaths or on damp sidewalls in bare soil.

Clubmosses *(cnwpfwsoglau)*

Clubmosses have been around for nearly 400 million years and as such are one of the oldest plant groups still found growing. They pre-date flowering plants by 275 million years. During the Carboniferous period (350 million years ago) they were the dominant plant life and are likely to have grown up to 30m tall. It is ancestral clubmoss which make up the bulk of organic material from which coal has formed.

Clubmosses have an inefficient method of reproduction, involving the release of spores into the open air. They have been out-competed by the more advanced seed plants. Today, clubmosses have retreated to the arctic alpine zone. They can be seen in the poor acidic soils of the Snowdonia uplands from about 400m above sea level. Above about 700m they become much more abundant. The succulent leaves of the clubmosses prevent them from drying out in the arid winds found at altitude. There are three types of clubmoss commonly found on the hills of Snowdonia; alpine clubmoss, fir clubmoss and stag's horn clubmoss.

Clubmosses have a lifecycle with two distinct generations. The visible plant above ground is the sporophyte which produces spores. These are in terminal cones *(strobili)* on stag's horn clubmoss and in fertile zones along the stem in fir clubmoss.

The spores of the clubmoss are homosporous, which means they produce bisexual free-living spores which live underground and feed on fungi. They then develop male and female organs and reproduce; this stage can take up to fifteen years.

Fir clubmoss can spread by producing disc shaped vegetative propagules and stag's horn clubmoss can spread by means of creeping stems *(stolons)*.

Fir clubmoss (*Huperzia selago*).

Alpine clubmoss
(*Diphasiastrum alpinium*).

Stag's horn clubmoss
(*Lycopodium clavatum*).

Foliose or leaf-like.

Crustose or crust-like.

Fruticose or shrub-like.

LICHENS

Lichen (*cen* in Welsh) is amazing stuff. It has a greater latitudinal and altitudinal range than any other organism on the planet. It is a year-round companion in the mountains from sea level to summit. When all the leaves and flowers have gone, lichen will be there to brighten up the day. They need clean air to grow and can be used as a monitor of air quality. The mountains of Snowdonia provide an excellent environment for lichen to thrive.

Lichen is an unusual organism; actually, it is a combination of two organisms, a symbiotic relationship between a fungus and an alga. The fungus grows around the alga to protect and shelter it in places where it would normally be washed away by heavy rains. Algae, unlike fungi, can photosynthesize (draw energy from the sun). Fungi tend to live on organic matter such as dead wood or faeces. The algae help to sustain the fungi and allow it to grow in places where fungi cannot normally grow, on the bare rocky faces to be found all over the mountains of Snowdonia.

Unfortunately, identifying lichen can be quite difficult (there are over 1,800 species of lichen in the UK). To identify different species sometimes involves microscopic inspection or even acid tests. To further the difficulties, few lichens have common names and even their scientific names have changed over the years. Lichens can be grouped into different types by their appearance; those most likely to be seen on the hill include foliose (leaf-like), crustose (crust-like) and fruticose (shrub-like).

Allantoparmelia alpicola.

Aspicilia contorta.

Allantoparmelia alpicola

Allantoparmelia means 'sausage-shaped parmelia' after the in-folded lobes. This is the only species of this genus in the UK. This dark-brown to black lichen likes well-lit rocks in mountainous regions, usually above 600m.

Aspicilia contorta

Aspicilia means 'cilate sheild'. Cilate describes the torn margins of the older fruiting bodies. This lichen is not widespread, but its warty texture is quite distinctive. The fruity bodies look like small volcanic islands with black discs raised on small cones. It is found on hard limey rocks.

Bloody-eye lichen *(Ophioparma ventosa)*

Formerly identified within the genus *Haematomma*, this is a common grey crustose lichen which covers the acid rocks of our uplands. 'Ophioparma' means snake-like shield, from the serpentine undulations on the fruiting bodies (too small to see with the naked eye). The fruiting bodies, however, stand out as blood-red discs in the middle of the grey mass of the lichen. It grows on exposed hillside rocks in areas which are nutrient deficient. It is also found on the old dry stone walls of long-abandoned settlements.

Cladonia callosa

Previously known as *C. fragilissima*, this lichen can be spotted on moorland often in peaty areas. It comprises flat leaf-like structures called squamules which are between 3mm and 6mm wide.

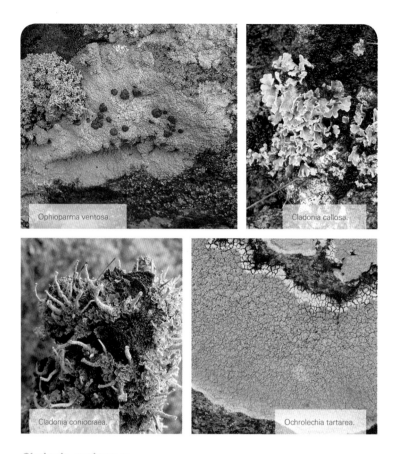

Ophioparma ventosa.

Cladonia callosa.

Cladonia coniocraea.

Ochrolechia tartarea.

Cladonia coniocraea

The stalk-like structures of this lichen are called podetia and can grow up to 3cm tall. It can be found in most woodland, growing on decaying stumps and logs. However, it can also grow on stone and is often seen on the walls of ancient enclosures on the hill. This is one of the few pollution-resistant lichens so can also be seen in urban areas.

Cudbear lichen *(Ochrolechia tartarea)*

This is a common grey crustose lichen. Usually found in exposed areas with high rainfall, it can be seen covering the rocks of mountain tops. It has been used as a source of crimson or purple dye.

Cladonia floerkeana.

Peltigera membranacea.

Devil's matchstick *(Cladonia floerkeana)* *(pennau matsys)*

This is the classic devil's matchstick lichen. There are several species for which the top to the podetia is red or orange, but this one is the most frequently seen. The red tips are the apothecia (fruiting bodies) of the fungal component of this lichen. It does vary quite a lot, but can usually be seen as a rough textured grey stalk between 1cm and 2cm high. It grows on rotting wood, in humus and on peat.

Dog Lichen *(Peltigera membranacea)* *(tafod y ci)*

Peltigera means 'shield-carrying' and this describes the shape of the fruiting bodies (apothecia). This is one of the larger-lobed lichens with the body of the lichen up to 25cm in diameter. It is grey when dry and brown when wet and will be found in open damp meadows. Sometimes called dog lichen as it resembles the much rarer *P. canina* which is found on impoverished dunes and sandy soils and not on the mosses, trees and rocks of Snowdonia favoured by *P. membranacea*.

Hypogymnia physodes

This lichen looks very similar to some of the Parmelia species. It does have some structural differences which will not be apparent to the non-expert. It grows on trees, rocks, moss and on heather stems. It is resistant to acid and is actually in decline as acid rain decreases.

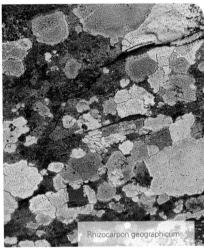

Hypogymnia physodes.

Rhizocarpon geographicum.

Map lichen *(Rhizocarpon geographicum) (cwilt y mynydd)*

This crustose lichen is easily spotted growing on the sunny acidic rocks across the high mountains of Snowdonia. Its bright yellow colour makes it stand out well and fun can be had trying to read the maps (created by its cracked appearance and the black encircling outline). The fruiting bodies are the small black discs. The thallus (the whole body of the lichen) can vary in size from a couple of centimetres across to about 20cm across.

Lichenometry

Map lichen can be useful to climatologists when assessing the relative age of exposed rock such as might be found in a moraine, a clue to the history of a receding glacier. By measuring the maximum size on rocks of a known age in similar climates (gravestones, buildings and well studied moraines) then, if the largest patch of lichen growing on a rock is the oldest, a comparison can be made to determine the minimum exposure time of the rock.

Parmelia caperata

Parmelia means 'embedded fruit bowl', owing to the appearance of the fruiting bodies nestling within the folds of this lichen. It's a large lichen covering an area of up to 20cm across, with its lobes of 1cm. When dry it is a yellow-green colour and a distinctive light green when wet. Often found on the bark of trees, it also appears on well-lit rocks and growing over mosses.

Parmelia saxatilis

This is one of the larger broad-leaved foliose lichens common throughout Britain, which can be found on rocks, stone walls and trees. It has been used as a wool dye to produce a reddish-brown colour. It is also traditionally thought to have medicinal qualities and the most-prized specimens were said to grow on the skulls of hanged men!

Peltigera polydactyla

Smaller leaved than *P membranacea*, and commonly found in mossy areas.

Pixie cup lichen *(Cladonia fimbriata & C. pyxidata)* *(cylch y cerrig)*

C. fimbriata has podetia up to 15mm tall which are topped off with a smooth rounded cup. It is commonly found on rotting wood, in earth, in humus on walls and among mosses. It can also withstand pollution.

C. pyxidata has a much rougher texture than *C. fimbriata* but otherwise looks very similar. It is the same height and colour. It was once used to produce a remedy for whooping cough. It grows on mossy trees, on rocks and in walls and is very common.

Parmelia caperata (and closeup inset).

Parmelia saxatilis.

Peltigera polydactyla.

Cladonia fimbriata.

Cladonia pyxidata.

Cladonia portentosa.

Cladonia rangiferina.

Lasallia pustulata.

Reindeer Moss *(Cladonia portentosa & C. rangiferina)* *(cen y carw)*

C. portentosa grows in light-coloured branched fruticose mats up to 6cm high, usually white to light-green grey in colour (although it can exhibit a purple-brown tinge). The typical 'model railway tree' lichen. It's very common on heaths and peat moors (although it may be in decline). It was formerly known as *Cladonia impexa*.

C. rangiferina is similar to *C. portentosa* but has smaller branch angles, giving it a more droopy appearance. It can form thick mats up to 8cm tall. It is more common in Scotland but can also be found in moorland and by the coast. Named after the Latin for reindeer, *Rangifer tarandus*.

Rock tripe *(lasallia pustalata)*

Quite often seen on sunny rocks in the hills. A large luxuriant growth is indicative of clean air. The thallus (body of the lichen) will be in the region of 6cm diameter, but it grows in large clusters. It can be eaten if boiled then fried with oat meal and has also been used in dyeing.

Rhizocarpon hochstetteri

This crustose lichen can form quite large circles, sometimes up to 15cm across. Its colour varies from dark-brown to grey and it is cracked into regular plates. The tiny fruiting bodies are the black bits which are less than 1mm across. It is not very common, but can be seen in the uplands on less acidic rocks.

Rhizocarpon hochstetteri.

Stereocaulon vesuvianum.

Usnea flammea.

Usnea florida.

Stereocaulon vesuvianum

Stereocaulon means 'sturdy stalk', evident in this light-grey lichen. It is very common on the high ground and can be seen in dense mats across well-lit acidic rocks growing up to 3cm high. It is equally happy on old dry stone walls or blocky bedrock, but there can also be great profusions of it around some of the older slate quarries.

Usnea flammea

This soft hair-like lichen can be seen growing on trees in the dense ancient woodlands found in Snowdonia's valleys. It has been used to treat uterine complaints, to arrest haemorrhaging and also as a source of glucose.

Usnea florida

A delicate bushy lichen found on trees, as can be seen near Cobden's Bridge in Capel Curig, and also on fence posts. It is similar to *U. flammea* but with distinctive shallow cup-shaped discs which are the spore-producing bodies.

Common shrew © K.M.Trivett www.flickr.com/keithtrivett

Diggings, evidence of small mammals.

Fox scat. Fur and bones from some unlucky small rodent can be made out. Note the pointed ends

MAMMALS

Small mammals

They are present in the hills all year round but most are very difficult to spot. Occasionally a flash of brown can be seen as a mouse or vole disappears from view, disturbed by your footsteps. Evidence of these small mammals can sometimes be seen in the form of diggings in grassland.

The larger mammals such as mountain ponies, feral goats and sheep are less easily startled. Foxes are also abundant in the hills, although you are more likely to see them in your home town. Fox scat can be found on the hillside as evidence of their presence. Foxes mark out their large territories by leaving scat on small mounds along the boundaries. Closer inspection will give some idea of the last meal the animal ate.

Common shrew *(Sorex araneus)* *(llŷg cyffredin)*

The only evidence you can usually see are little tunnels in the grass or crafted hollows and tiny holes. The shrew is constantly on the search for insects and other invertebrates. It is about 7.5cms long with a tail about half the length of the body and a distinctive pointed snout. Although rarely seen it is common in hedgerows, marshes, woods and meadows.

Large mammals

Welsh mountain ponies *(Equus caballus)* **(merlen mynydd)**
These are one of the more delightful sights of the Carneddau. They can be seen all year round but stand out more in the winter when they come down off the high tops. Although they live a free and wild life, their numbers are controlled by people. There are a couple of farms in the Carneddau who 'own' the ponies and every now and then they cull a good number to maintain a healthy breeding stock.

Feral goats *(Capra hircus)* **(gafr wyllt)**
Groups of goats can be a spectacular sight when out and about in the Glyderau or around Beddgelert. In dry weather, they are often to be found low down looking for water or being tempted by the many tasty plants found in gardens which border the open hillside. Goats are particularly damaging to woodland, stripping bark and destroying new growth. In recent years, there seems to have been a rise in the number of goats to be found on the hill. It would appear that the milder winters and reduction in sheep numbers have been beneficial to the goat population. Such is the concern about the increase in numbers that some culls have taken place. Many visitors may be disappointed to hear this, but it would be pointless reducing sheep numbers to increase biodiversity on the hill if goat numbers increase to take their place.

Goats were originally introduced to graze the steep areas of land unsuitable for sheep. Unfortunately for the farmers that introduced them, they proved uneconomical so were simply left to their own devices.

In spring, the female goats form a separate herd from the male goats. The nanny goats look after their kids, introducing them to their home turf (or heft). Meanwhile, gangs of Billy goats will roam far and wide looking for tasty food. This is when local gardens are under threat!

Sheep *(Ovis aries)* *(dafad)*

Wales is certainly famous for sheep and their presence has altered much of the landscape seen today. Since the Second World War, farmers have been subsidised according to the numbers of sheep they were grazing. This has maintained the grassland on the hills, making it easy and enjoyable to walk through them.

Unfortunately, sheep will eat any other tasty plants that choose to grow here and overgrazing has led to a rather monotonous monoculture. Today, farm subsidies are worked out on a land stewardship basis, meaning that sheep numbers have been reduced and there is more biodiversity on the hills. The downside of this is that when sheep grazing is reduced, the bracken and heather can take over which is not nearly so pleasant to walk through as sheep-cropped grass.

It will take experimentation to find a happy medium between having uplands pleasant, easy and interesting to walk through and those which are dominated by heather or bracken. There can be no denying the sight of gambolling lambs is one of the nicest we come across as we travel through Snowdonia towards the end of the winter season.

Feral goat.

Mountain pony.

Lambs on a farm outside Dolwyddelan.

SPRING

Barren strawberry.

Common lady's mantle in Cwm Idwal.

FLOWERS

Spring is the time for flowers on the hill. A large sample of the flowers seen while walking or climbing in Snowdonia follows. Note that the culinary and medicinal comments are included purely for interest; please do not pick wild flowers. It is in fact unlawful to uproot any plant from the wild without the landowner's consent; even collecting flowers or seeds from protected plants is illegal. The list below is roughly arranged by habitat type: rocky, grassy and wet or boggy.

Rocky areas

Barren strawberry *(Potentilla sterilis)* *(llwyn coeg-fefus)*

Barren strawberry is a low hairy perennial with white flowers, smaller and less erect than the true strawberry. It is widespread and common on dry ground and in woods. This example was seen growing in a crevice low on Craig Ddu in the Llanberis Pass. Unfortunately, its fruit is rather dry and quite unlike the real strawberry. This is reflected in the Welsh name which translates as 'empty strawberry shrub'.

Common lady's mantle *(Alchemilla vulgaris)* *(mantell Fair)*

This low-growing plant prefers calcareous soils so it is not widespread. Some can be found at the back of Cwm Idwal. Although not a particularly spectacular plant in itself, the raindrops it holds in its leaves are breathtakingly pretty. The young leaves can be eaten raw or cooked. They can be mixed with the leaves of bistort *(Polygonum bistorta)* and redleg *(Polygonum persicaria)* and used to make a bitter herb pudding called 'Easter ledger' which was eaten during Lent. The plant is rich in tannin and has been used both internally and externally in the treatment of wounds. It is said to stop vaginal discharge and has also been used as a treatment for excessive menstruation and to heal lesions after pregnancy. Prolonged use is said to ease the discomfort of the menopause, hence the name.

Globeflower *(Trollius europaeus)* *(cronnell)*

This is a spectacular member of the buttercup family which is highly localised. It will be familiar to anyone who has walked through an alpine meadow in June. In Wales, the plant hides away on rock ledges in areas with less acidic rock types. The back walls of Cwm Idwal can provide a spectacular display from May to August. Its flowers are wonderful golden orbs and the plant can reach up to 60cm high. The globeflower has been used as a purgative but loses its medicinal properties when dried.

Dwarf willow *(salix herbacea)* *(helygen leiaf)*

The dwarf willow looks nothing like a willow tree! This is a tiny creeping plant, with leaves only 1–2cm long and quite round. It is a true arctic-alpine species which is only found on higher ground, and is so low-growing that it appears as if the leaves are growing straight from the ground. It struggles to compete with other species, so will only be found on bare, exposed stony ground where other species neglect to grow. It appears to be relatively common amongst the cracked gabbro of the Cuillin on Skye. Rare in North Wales, this plant was photographed close to the summit of Y Garn where competition from other species is very limited.

Globeflower on Clogwyn y Geifr in Cwm Idwal.

Globeflower.

Dwarf willow on the summit of Y Garn.

Mossy saxifrage in the streambed above Twll Du in Cwm Idwal.

Mossy saxifrage *(Saxifraga hypnoides)* *(tormaen mwsoglaidd)*

This plant forms a moss-like mat which acts as protection from the drying winds found in higher areas. The flower protrudes up to 15cm. It is an arctic-alpine species which has adapted to life on stony ground and on small rock ledges. It can be seen in large quantities around the back of Cwm Idwal and alongside many streambeds on Snowdon.

Mountain sorrel in the scree of Cwm Idwal.

Purple saxifrage high in Cwm Tregalan.

Mountain sorrel *(Oxyria digyna) (suran y mynydd)*

Smaller than its common cousin, the mountain sorrel only grows on mountains. It can be seen in rocky places away from the heavily grazed parts of the mountain and grows to about 20cm high. The slightly acid-tasting leaves can be eaten raw, cooked or fermented into sauerkraut for winter use but take care; eat too much and it can bind up the calcium in the body which may then lead to nutrient deficiency.

Purple saxifrage *(Saxifraga oppositifolia) (tormaen porffor)*

Purple saxifrage bears beautiful little flowers which can appear as early as February in Snowdonia. It is another of the genuine arctic-alpine plants which grows low amongst rocks and on broken areas of cliff. It has adapted to survive under snow, then flower as soon as the snow melts. Purple saxifrage is a real treat in the wilder steeper areas of the Glyderau and Snowdon towards the end of the winter.

Roseroot *(Sedum rosea) (pren y ddannoedd)*

A strange succulent plant which is very susceptible to grazing, this arctic-alpine is confined to rocky ledges away from sheep and goats where it grows up to 30cm high. It has a wide range of medicinal properties, most interestingly as a stimulant which can be used to combat stress. *Dannoedd* means toothache in English, providing a clue to one of its past uses in Wales.

Roseroot.

Scurvy grass.

Scurvy grass *(Cochlearia officinalis)* *(llwylys cyffredin)*

Scurvy grass is widespread in coastal areas but is less common in the uplands. It has heart-shaped leaves and white flowers with four widely-spaced petals growing to a height of 20cm. Welsh shepherds are reputed to have eaten the leaves of this plant at one time as a vegetable to ward off scurvy, in a similar way to sailors. It can be seen in the upper reaches of Glyder Fawr, close to where the Idwal stream starts.

Starry saxifrage *(Saxifraga stellaris)* *(tormaen serennog)*

This is probably the most common saxifrage encountered in Snowdonia. It grows in wet flushes on the acidic soils which abound here and can be found in all the main mountain ranges. The two yellow spots near the base of each petal are very distinctive. It has crenulated hairy leaves and the flower grows to around 12cm high.

Starry saxifrage.

Thrift *(Armeria maritima)* *(clustog Fair)*

Much more common by the coast, the characteristic tufts of this plant can also be seen on rock ledges in the mountains which provide the same type of open exposed habitat. Gogarth climbers know the green part of the plant as 'astroturf'. It makes a comfortable seat, but does not have great properties as a hold. The delicate pink flowers protrude up to 20cm from the astroturf. The dried flower is an antibiotic which has been used to treat obesity, some nervous disorders and urinary infections.

Wall pennywort or navelwort *(Umbilicus rupestris)* *(deilen gron)*

This evergreen plant can grow in some quite ridiculous places. It can be seen inhabiting the slightest of cracks in cliffs faces. It is particularly abun-dant on the rocks at Tremadog. It also forms wonderful mini rock-gardens when it grows in moss beds on boulders. It varies greatly in size from just a few centimetres high to almost 40cm high with leaves more than 5cm across. The leaves can be eaten in a salad during springtime. A poultice of the leaves can be used to treat piles, burns or scalds. The Welsh name translates as buxom or round leaf.

Thrift on the sea cliffs of Anglesey, which can also be spotted in the mountains.

Pennywort at Tremadog.

Pennywort.

Wood sorrel, tucked into crevices on the Cwm idwal path.

Wood sorrel *(Oxalis acetosella)* *(suran y coed)*

Wood sorrel looks very much like clover until the bonny little flower appears, when it is then confused with the Snowdon lily! It is usually found in shady areas under rocks and grows to no more than 7–8cm high. Wood sorrel is, as its name suggests, a woodland indicator species. Where wood sorrel is found there were once trees; otherwise it grows in an environment of shade and shelter similar to woodland. The leaves, when fresh, taste like a strong green apple. They should be eaten sparingly, however, as they can bind up the calcium in the body leading to a nutrient deficiency.

Spring flowers of bilberry.

Grassy areas

Bilberry *(Vaccinium myrtillus)* *(llusen)*

This plant is well known and appreciated on all British uplands. The berries, which ripen in August, are delicious; the picture shows the flowers of the bilberry in spring. Bilberry has many local names such as blaeberry, whinberry, hurt and whortleberry. For some of its many uses and properties see page 110.

Bluebell *(Hyacinthoides non-scripta)* *(clychau'r gog)*

One of our most popular springtime flowers, bluebells are often seen carpeting woodlands. It is a woodland indicator species; where bluebells are seen there were once woods. Bluebells will often be found in areas of bracken, as the bracken offers essential shade to the bluebells and acts as a woodland surrogate. The name non-scriptus means 'unmarked' and refers to the plain blue petals which contrast with those of the hyacinth. The Welsh name *clychau'r gog* translates as cuckoo-bells since the plant flowers around the same time as the cuckoo is first heard in the springtime. The sap of bluebell stems and bulbs can be used as paper glue.

Common dog violet *(Viola riviniana)* *(fioled gyffredin)*

The dog violet is a beautiful little flower often found in woodlands and is common in grassy mountain places. The dog violet has another Welsh name: *sanau'r gwcw*, which translates as the cuckoo's socks as this plant also flowers around the time the first cuckoos are heard. Ancient folklore suggests that it is unlucky to pick these flowers in small bunches and that bringing a few into your house would stop your hens laying. In parts of Wales, the flowers were once collected and made into a treacle by adding water and sugar. This was once considered to be an unrivalled cure for colds, coughs and chest complaints.

Foxglove *(Digitalis purpurea)* *(bysedd y cŵn)*

Once in flower, this plant is immediately recognisable from the cottage gardens of old England and Wales. It can cause confusion before flowering, as its leaf base grows quite early in the year. Foxglove is famous for being poisonous. The Welsh name *bysedd y* cŵn translates as the 'dog's finger'. The foxglove does, however, have other names in Wales such as *gwniadur Mair* (Mary's thimble), demonstrating a strong devotion of rural Welsh people towards the Virgin Mary.

Bluebells on Clogwyn y Grochan in the Llanberis Pass.

Common dog violet.

Foxglove.

Heath bedstraw.

Heath bedstraw *(Galium saxatile)* *(briwydd y rhostir)*

Heath bedstraw bears small white flowers, abundant in grassy places from June until August. Heath bedstraw forms low, quite dense mats, well mixed with grass. It has a delicate fragrance which may not be to everyone's liking, but was once spread on stone floors to keep them sweet.

Heath speedwell *(Veronica officinalis)* *(rhwyddlwyn meddygol)*

This only grows in dry grassy places so is not a plant to be expected in Snowdonia. However, it has been found flourishing on the slopes above Llyn Teyrn. It has a characteristic hairy stalk ringed with delicate lilac flowers. It is a low-growing plant achieving no more than 20cm in height. A bitter tangy tea can be made from this flowering herb or the dried leaves can be added to tea blends. They have been used to treat kidney complaints, haemorrhages and skin diseases although herbalists would agree that it has been superseded by modern drugs.

Heath speedwell above the Miner's Path by Llyn Teyrn.

The flowers of milkwort vary in colour (above & right).

Milkwort *(Polygala vulgaris)* *(amlaethai cyffredin)*

Confusingly, its flowers come in blue, mauve, pink or white! The very small flower is common in both calcareous (lime rich) and acid (lime deficient) grassland areas. Although rarely growing above 15cm tall, it can reach 30cm tall. The leaves can be used as a tea substitute. Milkwort is thought to have sweat-inducing and diuretic properties. Its name comes from the (unproven) belief that it can increase the milk flow in nursing mothers.

Primrose *(Primula vulgaris)* *(briallen)*

The primrose is a beautiful and very common flower which is a favourite sign of spring. It can be abundant in woods and on hedgerows, but is also found dotted around the mountains. The flowers are edible and can be used to decorate a salad or fermented to make an intoxicating wine. Primroses have a very long history of medicinal use and have been used for treating conditions involving spasms, cramps, paralysis and rheumatic pains. Another Welsh name is *blodau llo bach*, the 'bloom of the little calf'.

Flowering primrose.

Tormentil.

Wild thyme next to the path in Cwm Idwal.

Tormentil *(Potentilla erecta)* *(tresgl y moch)*

This small yellow flower with four petals is a walker's constant companion in the hills from April until October. Tormentil is that little yellow flower seen in every grassy area on the hill. It is usually quite low on the heavily grazed hillsides, but can reach a metre in height in longer grass as it strives for sunlight. Although it looks a bit like a buttercup, it is actually a member of the rose family. A tea can be made from its roots, but it is not a particularly edible plant. However, its medicinal properties are legendary. It is well known for being a highly astringent herb which has been used as a cure for fever, diarrhoea, burns, cholera, dysentery, sore throats, irritable bowel syndrome, colitis, mouth ulcers, infected gums, piles, inflamed eyes, chapping of the anus, cracked nipples, bed-wetting by children and toothache. Its Latin name, however, suggests other properties!

Wild thyme *(Thymus polytrichus)* *(teim gwyllt)*

Wild thyme is very common in dry grassy areas, forming low-lying mats with short flowering stems and hairy leaves. Pick a few leaves and eat raw in salad or add as a flavouring to cooked food. If you choose to dry the leaves, pick them in early summer just before the flowers open. An aromatic tea can be made from the leaves or dried flowers. The leaves, and especially the essential oil contained within them, can be used as an antiseptic, antispasmodic, deodorant, disinfectant and sedative. The essential oil from the leaves can also be used in perfumery and soaps and the dried flowers can also be used to repel moths from clothing.

Cwm Idwal, a particularly good place to see bogbean in May and June.

Bogbean.

Butterwort.

Wet or boggy areas

Bogbean *(Menyanthes trifoliata)* *(ffeuen y gors)*

Bogbean is a very distinctive plant with spectacular flowers that project, along with the leaves, about 30cm above the water in ponds all around the hills. The roots can be cooked but must be treated to get rid of an acrid taste, which involves drying it out thoroughly, grinding it into a powder and then washing it in running water. Unfortunately, this treatment will also remove many of the vitamins and minerals contained in the root. The powder has been used for making famine bread, but the root can be used as an emergency food when all else fails! The bitter leaves can be used as a substitute for hops in making beer. Bogbean is closely related to the gentians, which are famous bitter herbs used as a digestive and general body tonic. This plant can be used similarly as it is anti-inflammatory, astringent, cathartic, digestive, diuretic and hypnotic, but it can irritate the digestive system of patients with gastric inflammation or infections. All parts of the plant are medically active, but the leaves are the part most commonly used. These are best used dried as the fresh plant causes vomiting. It is also believed to be a good remedy for rheumatoid arthritis, especially when this condition is associated with weakness, weight loss and lack of vitality. Note that excess doses can cause vomiting.

Butterwort *(Pinguicula vulgaris)* *(tafod y gors)*

Butterwort is a low, sticky perennial which grows in sunny nitrogen-deficient bogs. It has a beautiful blue flower which grows about 12cm above the starfish-like leaves. To supplement its diet, it traps insects on its sticky leaves and digests them. It is one of the two common insectivorous plants to be found around our uplands (the other being sundew). Its leaves were once used to curdle milk and have also been used as a laxative. The Welsh name, *tafod y gors*, translates as 'tongue of the bog'.

Common cottongrass
(Eriophorum angustifolium) *(plu'r gweunydd)*

Cottongrass is actually a sedge. It grows in acidic boglands up to 45cm high and is a good indicator of where not to walk! The leaves and roots have been used as a cure for diarrhoea. Attempts have been made to make a cotton substitute from the flower heads, but the hairs are too brittle and cannot be twisted. The dried leaves and stems have, however, been woven to make soft covers.

Hare's tail cottongrass
(Eriophorum vaginatum) *(plu'r gweunyd unben)*

Hare's tail cottongrass is very similar to common cotton grass, but grows in tussocks and only ever has a single flower spike.

Common cottongrass (and inset).

Hare's tail cottongrass.

Cross-leaved heath or
bog heather *(Erica tetralix)* **(grug croesddail)**
This is one of the three common heathers found in Snowdonia. Usually the first to flower, cross-leaved heath prefers wetter ground than the more common bell heather and ling. Its flowers are the same shape as those of bell heather, but they tend to be pinker and cluster around the heads of stalks. The leaves and stems are also a more sage green than those of the other heathers. There are no known edible or medicinal uses of this plant, but its stems can be used for making brooms and brushes and a yellow dye has been made from the plant.

Early purple orchid *(Orchis mascula)* **(tegeirian coch y gwanwyn)**
This is a common orchid in woodlands, but is seen less often in the mountains. It usually has spots or blotches on its leaves, but they are strangely absent from the Cwm Idwal specimens. When the root is cooked it is a source of 'salep'. This fine white substance is obtained by drying the tuber and grinding it; the resulting powder is a starch-like substance with a sweetish taste. It is said to be very nutritious and can be made into a drink or added to cereals. One ounce of salep is said to be enough to sustain a person for a day. Salep, being very nutritive, has been used as a diet of special value for children and convalescents.

Heath-spotted orchid
(Dactylorhiza maculata) **(tegeirian brych y rhos)**
This is a very common and easily distinguished orchid. It grows on damp acidic moorland soils and is easily recognised by the spots on its leaves and petals. As with the early purple orchid, salep can be made from the roots.

Ivy-leaved crowfoot
(Ranunculus hederaceus) **(crafanc-y-frân dail eiddew)**
Most crowfoots have submerged leaves but this type displays its ivy-shaped leaves above the water. It is one of the first flowers to be seen in March. It is poisonous.

Cross-leaved heath or bog heather.

Heath-spotted orchid.

An early purple orchid, in the back of Cwm Idwal, where they are common.

Ivy-leaved crowfoot spotted in fresh running water in Cwm Penmachno.

Lousewort *(Pedicularis sylvatica)* *(melog y cŵn)*

This is a small, semi-parasitic perennial which grows in damp and boggy places, often hiding in the grass. Once spotted, several more can be seen in the same area. It was once thought that grazing animals could catch liver-fluke from this pretty little plant; it is now known that fluke and lousewort flourish in similar locations.

Sundew *(Drosera rotundifolia)* *(gwlithlys)*

Visit any boggy area in the acidic uplands of Snowdonia from April onwards and you may well see this little beauty. It is characterised by its gorgeous sunshine-like leaves tipped with sticky globules, which it uses to catch insects. Like butterwort, this is a way of supplementing the diet of the plant which grows in nitrogen-deficient boggy areas. Towards the end of June and into August, it displays a pretty little white flower atop a slender stalk up to 18cm tall. Sundew can be used to curdle milk. The juice from the leaves is supposed to cure warts, corns and bunions. However, if the plant is ingested for one of it's many other medicinal properties such as curing whooping cough, chronic bronchitis and asthma, it can discolour your urine! The Welsh name translates as 'sun sweat'. It is also thought to be an aphrodisiac for cattle!

Water avens *(Geum rivale)* *(mapgoll glan y dŵr)*

Water avens are widespread and common on stream banks and other wet, shady places; however a keen eye is required to pick them out in the mountains. They grow in damp flushes on the rock ledges of Clogwyn y Geifr, amongst other places. They belong to the lily family and the leaves growing straight from the base of the plant have three parts. Water avens flower from May to September and are pollinated by bees. It grows to a height of 30cm. The dried or fresh root can be boiled in water to make an apparently delicious chocolate-like drink and it has been used to flavour ales in the past. The root is anti-inflammatory, antiseptic, aromatic, astringent and tonic. It is said that it can remove spots and freckles and that the dried root repels moths.

Wood anemone *(Anemone nemorosa)* *(blodyn y gwynt)*

Wood anemone is very common in woodlands where vast carpets can be found, but is much rarer in the mountains. It grows to a height of about 30cm. All anemones are referred to as wind flowers as, according to the Roman naturalist Pliny, they do not open until the wind blows. This is reflected in the Welsh name as *blodyn* means flower and *gwynt* means wind. It is inedible and the plant is not used by herbalists today, but the leaves are considered to be anti-rheumatic.

Lousewort on Crimpiau above Capel Curig.

Sundew with trapped insects on its sticky leaves.

Water avens.

Wood anemone spotted in a wet gully to the right of the Idwal Slabs.

Soaring buzzard.

Chough. Photograph
Jim Krawiecki.

MOUNTAIN BIRDS

To be perfectly honest, our hills and mountains are not the best place for bird watching. Birds are few and far between, however this makes it much easier to identify the ones we do see! To hear the birdcalls visit www.rspb.org.uk; this is a fantastic website with video and audio footage of all British birds. As with all these sites, however, it's easier to look up a bird if you know what it is first. The birds most likely to be seen in the hills and mountains of Snowdonia are as follows.

Buzzard *(Buteo buteo)* **(bwncath)**

If it's big it's a buzzard! The buzzard is our most common bird of prey and is also one of the largest. In silhouette, its large broad, rounded wings with a short neck and tail are evident. The call is a distinctive 'mew'. The buzzard lives off small birds and mammals up to the size of a large rabbit. It is not adverse to the odd bit of carrion and can often be seen circling on the air currents close to roads through the higher parts of the national park. In common with other birds of prey, the female of the species is larger than the male; they can weigh over 1kg and stand over 50cm tall.

Chough *(Pyrrhocorax pyrrhocorax)* **(bran goesgoch)**

The chough is a little beauty, nationally quite rare but abundant in small pockets of Snowdonia. It is easily distinguished from the larger raven by its size, its call and the fact that it is a much more sociable bird, often seen engaging in group aerobatics particularly in the spring and autumn. Look out for its distinctive red beak and legs. The call is a piercing 'cheeow'. They sustain themselves with small insects and worms. A full-grown chough will be 40cm tall and weigh around 300g.

Dipper *(Cinclus cinclus)* **(bronwen y dŵr)**

A small stout bird, 18cm long, with a bright white chest. It is often seen in fast-flowing streams and easily recognised by its 'bobbing' characteristic while standing on midstream rocks as it feeds on water-borne invertebrates. It has a loud 'clink' call that features some warbling notes mixed in with louder single notes. The nest is quite a bulky dome shape made from moss and grass, and is located in steep river banks or under bridges.

Herring gull *(Larus argentatus)* **(gwylan y penwaig)**

The large seagull which is all too commonly seen in the hills. As soon as your packed lunch is opened a herring gull will appear, especially on Snowdon or the Glyderau. They have even been seen raiding the rucksacks of climbers on Dinas Mot, cleverly waiting until the climbers are a pitch up their route. To many, they are the 'rats of the sky' and have no place in these uplands. They will, however, settle anywhere where there is food available for easy scavenging. Walkers and climbers who feed them and leave apple cores in the hills are to blame for them moving into the mountains, a few miles from the Welsh coast. They will nest on difficult to access open ground and can be seen rearing chicks on some of the small islands found in the Moelwynion lakes such as Llyn Edno. Love them or loath them, they have to be admired as beautiful effortless flyers.

Dipper.

Herring Gull high in the mountains of Snowdonia.

A cheeky jackdaw on the Great Orme.

Jackdaw *(Corvus monedula)* *(jac-y-do)*

Jackdaws are more likely to be found around villages in Snowdonia. There is a large population in Llanberis, but climbers will be most familiar with them from climbing at Tremadog. They are one of the more handsome crows, are very sociable and have a distinctive chatter. They swoop around in flocks at the start and end of the day, then let off a real cacophony as they settle down to roost in the evenings. They can be seen wandering about in twos or threes looking for insects, worms or leftover human scraps. A fully grown jackdaw stands about 30cm tall.

Kestrel *(Falco tinnunculus)* *(cudyll coch)*

Our most common bird of prey is just as likely to be spotted alongside the roadside as on the mountains. It has a pale underside, reddish brown back and a grey tail. It is most distinctive when hovering, as it is the only British bird which can hover in a stationary position while hunting for small mammals and large insects. It doesn't like completely open ground and can often be seen perched in trees or on poles on the edge of open moorland. The kestrel is about 32cm tall, with the male weighing an average 220g and the female 260g.

Meadow pipit *(Anthus pratensis)* *(corhedydd y waun)*

The meadow pipit is the most common songbird in the hills. They can frequently be seen in pairs fluttering about in acrobatic style over grassy areas. They are only 14cm long and weigh no more than 25g. Their nests can be found in spring by keeping eyes peeled and noting where they first take off from; they are, of course, trying to lead you away. The meadow pipit appears yellowish close up and the white of the outer tail feathers can often be seen in flight. It lives on insects and small seeds, and will move to lower ground in the winter.

Peregrine falcon *(Falco peregrinus)* *(hebog tramor)*

Peregrine falcons were rare but are now quite common in the uplands of Snowdonia. They often nest on high north-facing vegetated cliffs. Quite tolerant of human activity, they are still heavily protected and approaching their nests is definitely illegal. They can give some very exciting flying displays in the high cwms. During their swooping dive to catch small birds, they can achieve speeds of over 200 miles per hour. The loud bang accompanying a peregrine falcon taking out another bird is quite unforgettable. Their call is a loud screech. They are a dark grey colour and are easily recognised by their pointed wings. The female is around 46cm tall while the male is only 40cm. The male weighs an average 700g and the female will be 300–400g heavier. The Welsh name translates as 'foreign hawk'.

Kestrel 'covering' its prey.
Photograph by Andrew Chambers.

Meadow pipit.
© iStockphoto.com

Meadow pipit nest and (inset) eggs.

Peregrine falcon at site of kill.
© iStockphoto.com

Pied wagtail *(Motacilla alba)* *(siglen fraith)*

The pied wagtail is a common bird but is not usually seen on the uplands. It is, however, a frequent visitor to car parks. It will be easily recognised at the Pen y Pass and Ogwen car parks, walking around with its tail bobbing up and down looking for scraps. It is usually a black and white bird with a finely shaped long tail, although its colour can vary. It is also known as the white wagtail. The pied wagtail will be less than 20cm tall and weighs a little over 20g.

Raven *(Corvus corax)* *(cigfran)*

The raven is easily the most observed bird in the uplands at any time of the year. This large black bird, over 60cm from the tip of its tail to the end of its beak and weighing up to 1.5kg, has a distinctive throaty call rather like a strangled gargle. Reputedly very intelligent, they build large nests on south-facing cliff ledges. Young ravens can be found in large numbers around Newborourgh Warren on Anglesey in the autumn, where they travel to find a mate. The birds then pair up for life and return to make a permanent home on the high cliffs of Snowdonia. They will kill rabbits and smaller birds, but carrion such as young lambs is their staple diet. The Welsh name *cigfran* is celebrated across Snowdonia by numerous crags named Clogwyn y Cigfran.

Red Grouse *(Lagopus lagopus)* *(grugiar goch)*

Grouse is much less common in Snowdonia than the Pennines due to the lack of privately-owned shooting moors. Abandoned shooting butts can be found in the eastern areas of Snowdonia, but grouse are only seen infrequently. The best place to catch sight and sound of them is probably in the Moelwynion. Their loud sharp call when disturbed in the heather can startle. Their favourite food is heather shoots, hence the controlled burning of moorland in other upland areas.

Pied wagtail.

Raven. © iStockphoto.com

Raven's nest.

Red grouse.
© iStockphoto.com

Red kite.

Red kite *(Milvus milvus)* *(barcud)*

The red kite can be recognised by its red underbelly, long slender wings and deeply forked tail. It is quite a large bird, up to 60cm tall with the female weighing over 1kg and the male slightly less. In 1903, the red kite was considered a common bird. Its numbers were dramatically reduced throughout the 20th century by egg collectors, inadvertent poisoning, a decline in the rabbit population due to myxamatosis and extermination because of the threat they pose to poultry, partridge, grouse and pheasant. Tolerant of human presence and reliant on discarded meat and carrion, kites have been an easy target. Mid-Wales became its last refuge and the red kite became a symbol of southern Snowdonia. They are on the increase today, but are more likely to be seen in the Chilterns (where they have been successfully re-introduced). They have been spotted as far north as Blaenau Ffestiniog. Surprisingly, the red kite is not an upland bird by choice. In Tudor times they were common in London and other towns and they are most at home in the English Lowlands.

Ring ouzel *(Turdus torquatus)* *(mwyalchen y mynydd)*

Ring ouzels migrate to Snowdonia in March and April. They are very reminiscent of a blackbird, being around the same size, but are much greyer and have a distinctive white collar. Like the peregrine, this is a species which has increased in numbers significantly in recent years and can often be spotted on areas of rough moorland. There, they will be searching out a wide range of invertebrates and eating berries while nesting in the heather. The Welsh name translates as the mountain blackbird.

Sandpiper *(Actitis hypoleucos)* *(pibydd y dorlan)*

The sandpiper is a large bird with a brown back, pale front and black wing tips. It is a wader which bobs vigorously and can be seen flying low over water with rather shallow wing beats. The sandpiper will often be seen near mountain streams feeding on small invertebrates, Cwm Idwal being a particularly good place. It is 20cm long and weighs around 50g..

Skylark *(Alauda arvensis)* *(ehedydd)*

Skylarks are often heard but rarely seen. They have a fawn chest and a black and brown mottled back and can grow to 18cm tall and 40g in weight. It flies high in the air constantly singing its distinctive chirpy song, before diving down to swoop on pray. It is usually found above grassy areas where it hunts insects and builds its nest in grassy hummocks. When scavenging for food it bobs up and down, in flight it has very stiff wings and will give a distinctive three-note call as it takes off.

Ring ouzel, Photograph, Mark Walport.

Sandpiper.

Skylark with a captive insect in its beak.

Stonechat *(Saxicola torquatus)* *(clochdar y cerrig)*

The stonechat is a small sparrow-sized bird with distinctive colouring and an even more recognisable call. They have an orange breast, a brownish back and white cheeks; the males have a black head. They are often found in rocky areas on open moorland or darting around on the edge of gorse bushes. Their call is rather like two stones being knocked together.

Wheatear *(Oenanthe oenanthe)* *(tinwen y garn)*

The wheatear is a common summer visitor to the grassy areas of our uplands. It can be confused with meadow pipits, but will usually be solitary. It has a grey back, a buff chest and a striking black and white tail pattern. It was the flash of white in the tail which led to its original Saxon name of 'white arse'. The wheatear has a varied warbling song and will often be seen walking around in grassy areas or flitting around gorse bushes looking for insects. It is not very large, and is only about 15cm tall and never heavier than 30g.

Wren *(Troglodytes troglodytes)* *(dryw)*

The wren is Britain's most common breeding bird and is found just about everywhere including the mountains. It is another bird which is more often heard than seen. It has a loud, prolonged and musical call which can be heard all year round. It is tiny, never more than 12cm long, and this is the best way to recognise it as it flits in and out of areas of dense vegetation such as heather or bramble; indeed, it is Britain's smallest bird. It will nest deep in this dense vegetation, building a domed nest from twigs, moss hair and feathers.

Stonechat.

Wheatear.
© iStockphoto.com

Wren.
© iStockphoto.com

Frog and (inset) spawn and tadpoles.

Toad (© iStockphoto.com) and and (inset) toad spawn © Ashley Pinnock tinyurl.com/p7udrh

AMPHIBIANS & REPTILES

Grouped here for convenience, amphibians and reptiles are only superficially similar; cold-blooded vertebrates who hibernate through the winter and reappear in spring. Characteristically, amphibians go through a metamorphosis from aquatic young into air breathing adults.

Amphibians

Frog *(Rana temporaria)* *(llyffant melyn)*

Mostly to be seen in damp woods and meadows, they will usually be found sitting around on hillsides during the spring, just after mating. Frogs return annually to the sites where they were born and produce up to 4,000 eggs (frogspawn). Any shallow pool will do and frogspawn is often seen on dry ground where rainwater had lain for a few days. The frogspawn floats at the surface to get the sun's warmth. As they hatch, the tadpoles eat the spawn before turning to algae, which they survive on until they are big enough to take small insects. Most tadpoles will be eaten by fish or birds; five in every 2,000 may survive. Those that survive to become frogs can live for up to eight years. The adult frog can breathe through its skin as well as its nostrils. Useful adaptations when they are buried under piles of leaves for their hibernation or when they are sitting in water with their bodies covered. In the villages of Snowdonia, the local youngsters refer to a frog as *y broga*.

Toad *(Bufo bufo)* *(llyffant dafadennog)*

The warts across their backs differentiate toads from frogs. Toads can live up to 40 years. Like frogs, toads actually live away from water, usually in woodlands. They hibernate from October, typically under leaf litter or timber piles. They will emerge in late March and head for their breeding sites. Toadspawn differs from frogspawn as it is arranged in lines rather than a large mass. It will usually be hidden amongst waterweeds.

Reptiles

Adder *(Vipera berus)* *(gwiber)*

The only snake that can be found as far north as the Arctic Circle. They will most often seen on warm, sunny, spring days when they bask in the sun after coming out of hibernation in grassland on the edges of woodland. Adders (sometimes known as vipers) can grow to just over 80cm long on a varied diet of mice, voles, shrews, lizards and frogs. Adders themselves are preyed upon by buzzards but are protected from humans by law. Famed for their venomous bite, they are the only poisonous snake in the British Isles. Whilst bites are not uncommon, deaths from adder bites are rare; even so you should seek medical attention if bitten. Biting you is their last line of defence, so first they will try some pretty dramatic hissing.

Emerging from winter hibernation in April, there will be a lot of activity as the males search out females, wrestling with each other (the 'dance' of the adders) to see off smaller males. The male adder has a quite bright white or grey body with a black zigzag down their back whilst the female has a brown body with a dark brown zigzag.

The adder has been revered in Wales for its curative properties. Dried adder skins were thought to cure rheumatism and headaches whilst powdered adder skin, added to soup, was thought to cure constipation. Scurvy and bad skin conditions could be cured by letting live adders move over the afflicted areas and anyone who ate the flesh of white snake would be able to understand animal languages!

Adder.

Common lizard.
© iStockphoto.com

Common lizard *(Zootoca vivipara)* *(madfall)*

The common lizard likes open habitat such as moorland, grassland or quarries. The best time to see them is when they are basking in the warm spring sun. They are very alert and, despite being common, sightings are infrequent as they sense your presence and scurry for cover. The male common lizard ends its hibernation in March with the females beginning to appear in April when mating begins to take place. The female will then give birth to live young in July. The eggs in which they have begun life break as they are being born and this 'live' birth gives rise to the name vivipara which means 'live birth'. The young are born jet black then turn copper before developing their adult colour. Adult males have a bright underside, usually yellow or orange, which is densely covered in black spots whilst the females are yellow, grey or green on the underside but with few or no spots. Common lizards can be between 10 and 15cm long and live for up to 12 years. The common lizard feeds predominantly on spiders and small insects but when attacked by predators itself it can shed its tail. The tail does grow back but the lizard will have a scar for life. Better known in North Wales as *gennau goeg.*

The frog hopper larvae protects itself with a covering of froth. (Inset) the larvae.

Golden ringed dragonfly.

INSECTS

It is beyond the scope of this book to identify the many insects out there, but we have attempted to include examples of the most important. For convenience I have included spiders here even though they are arachnids.

Frog hopper *(Philaenus spumarius)* **(llyffant y gwair)**
The frog hopper could not be omitted. It is actually the larvae of the frog hopper which many are familiar with, also known as cuckoo spit. Frog hoppers are named for their truly remarkable jumping abilities; this 5mm long insect is able to jump distances of up to 70cm. A jump like this will produce a G-force of 500 times the force of gravity; this is 100 times more than an astronaut being propelled into space.

Golden ringed dragonfly *(Cordulegaster boltonii)*
This is an easily recognised dragonfly with its very distinctive yellow bands. It will be around 60cm long. It breeds near running water but can be found across the high ground often quite far from where it breeds. It is most active between May and September.

Garden spider. (Inset) garden spider webs in soft rush behind Plas Cwm y Llan

Spiders *(prif copyn)*

Many spiders can be seen on the hill during the springtime; if not the spiders, then their webs. There are around 640 named species of spider in Britain, of which over 300 are no more than 3mm long.

Garden spider *(Araneus diadematus)*
This is probably our most familiar spider. It is very common and widespread across many environments. It weaves beautiful webs which are often seen in patches of soft rush on the uplands. It will be up to 12mm long but the larger ones are females. The males being only 4 to 8mm long are occasionally mistaken for prey by the females. Look out for the white dots on the abdomen and transverse white streaks which meet to form a cross.

Beetles *(chwilen)*

Half of the world's biomass is insects and half of the insect biomass is beetles; that's a lot! Many of them are microscopic and live in the soil. There are many beetle species which may be encountered when out on the hills, a few of which are included here.

Reed beetle below Clogwyn y Tarw, Cwm Idwal.

Click beetle.

Ground beetle.

Reed beetle *(Plateumaris discolor)*

Most reed beetles are lowland species but the *Plareumaris discoulor* makes its home on the stems of cotton grass in the uplands. This bright metallic beetle can grow to 3cm long. It chooses to live in the oxygen-less environment of the bogs where cottongrass grows, to cope with this environment it has two spines which it uses to penetrate air pockets within the grass itself. The beetle will breathe like this through the winter then emerge in June.

Click beetle *(Ctenicera cuprea)*

This beetle is absent from the south-east of England and prefers to live on the rough grassland of upland areas. The larvae will live on roots and other small creatures found in the soil. They make a clicking sound when they jump. They have the strange ability to jump back up whether they land on their front or back; indeed, they will continue jumping until they land on their feet. They can grow up to 9mm long.

Ground beetle *(Cychrus caraboides)*

This is a beetle of woodland habitats, but is often seen on heather moorland too. It is up to 20cm long and feeds on snails by plunging its narrow front end into their shells to eat the flesh.

Dor beetle in Cwm Tregalan on Snowdon.

Longhorn beetle on the summit ridge of Moel Siabod.

Minotaur beetle near Capel Curig in February.

Rose chafer

Dor beetle *(Geotrupes stercorarius)*

Common across the whole of the UK, this beetle is one of our largest dung beetles. They are so named because they eat dung! They are therefore usually found close to cow dung where the females like to burrow underneath and then fill the tunnels with fresh dung on which their offspring can feast.

Longhorn beetle *(Rhagium bifasciatum)*

This is another widespread beetle, which favours decaying coniferous timber as its habitat. This example was photographed during a period of high pressure in June when rising air currents had lifted this beetle (and several million other irritating insects) up on to the summit ridge of Moel Siabod.

Minotaur beetle *(Typhaeus typhoeus)*

The Minotaur beetle can be recognised by its horns. It burrows under various kinds of dung and its tunnel can be up to 150cm deep. It grows up to 2cm long and can be active at any time of the year.

Rose chafer *(Cetonia aurata)*

This bright coppery green beetle flies quite noisily during the day from May to September but spends most of its time nibbling pollen and sipping nectar. It is usually between 15 and 20mm long. The larvae live and feed in rotting timber whilst the adult beetle will often be seen on flowers, especially roses. Whilst it is currently quite widespread it is thought to be in decline.

Snowdon beetle *(Chrysolina cerealis)* (not illustrated)

A small, 5 to 10mm long, brightly coloured beetle with red, gold and green striped body. In Continental Europe it is known as the rainbow leaf beetle. The beetle's main food is wild thyme and the adult beetle will lays its eggs in the grass nearby. Although good habitat for the beetle is quite common in Snowdonia it has only been spotted in a couple of locations on Snowdon; keep your eyes peeled and you may be lucky! It is quite common throughout Europe from Northern Italy to Norway, though only in small areas. In Snowdonia it is threatened by sheep grazing and climate change.

Violet ground beetle *(Carabus violaceus)*

As the name suggests the smooth body of this dark beetle has a violet tinge that often become coppery towards the edges. It can be seen all year round in many different habitats but is mostly active at night when it hunts for slugs. It grows up to 30mm long and as such is one of our largest beetles, and is often seen on the hill.

Violet ground beetle spotted on the way to Crimpiau above Capel Curig.

Moths, butterflies and caterpillars

Moths *(gwyfynod)* are closely related to butterflies *(gloynnod byw)*. The differences are small; in the shape and structure of the antenna, the wing coupling, the pupae and the body shape. Moths are usually less brightly coloured than butterflies. Both are caterpillars *(lindys)* as larvae.

Broom moth caterpillar *(Melanchra pisi)*
The broom moth caterpillar is very distinctive with three bold yellow strips. The body can vary from dark green to purplish brown. It is often found in bracken, brambles and heather. It is usually about 45mm long and will be seen on the hill between July and October. The broom moth itself is quite hard to spot having a rust colouring, and may be seen during the period from May to July.

Cream wave moth *(Scopula floslactata)*
Common across Wales and usually associated with deciduous forest.

Fox moth caterpillar *(Macrothylacia rubi)*
This is a very common sight from springtime onwards. The fox moth lives on heaths and grasslands and is partial to bramble. The caterpillar will often be seen in grassy areas. The moth is a buff brown colour with two pale wavy strips on each wing.

Small heath *(Coenonympha pamphilus)*
The small heath butterfly can be seen on finely leaved grasses between July and August. It will usually be busily darting around when it is sunny and is rarely seen at rest. When it does pause it always closes its wings and usually pulls its forewings down to conceal the eye-spot on each wing.

Wood tiger *(Parasemia plantaginis)*
Very distinctive. This moth can be spotted in areas of heath or scrubby grassland. The male flies by day but the female is nocturnal.

Broom moth caterpillar spotted in Cwm y Llan.

Cream wave moth found near the north side of Moel Siabod.

Fox moth caterpillar.

Small heath butterfly at rest on the shores of Llyn Idwal.

Wood tiger moth spotted in Cwm Eigiau in the Carneddau.

SUMMER

Bell heather.

Bell heather.

FLOWERS

Many of the flowers identified in the previous chapter are still in flower in the summer. Included here are those plants which come into flower a little later, usually in July, although one or two of them will make themselves known by the end of June. Hopefully you will have gained some familiarity with spring flowers and anything new in August can be found here.

Bell heather *(Erica cinerea) (grug y mel)*

Bell heather is common across moorland areas where grazing has been kept to a minimum; sheep love the little *Erica* shoots. Bell heather is an evergreen which erupts in flower towards the end of June and grows up to 45cm high. The purple bell-shaped flowers are a popular sight and an indicator of dry ground. All heathers are good producers of nectar and heather clumps are favourite haunts for bees. Look out for the heath bumblebee *(Bombus jonellus)* recognisable by its white rear end.

Bilberry *(Vaccinium myrtillus) (Ilusen)*

The little pink flowers of bilberry in spring are often mistaken for unripe berries. As August draws nearer, these flowers are replaced by wonderfully tasty berries much loved by people and birds. Help yourself to as many as you can eat, take some home and mix with apple for a wonderful pie. They are good for varicose veins, haemorrhoids and capillary fragility. Look out for the bilberry bumblebee *(Bombus monticola)*. This is an upland species of bee confined to areas of bilberry moor and is recognisable by its orange rear end.

Heath bumblebee.

Summer bilberry.

Common bird's foot trefoil alongside the Watkin Path.

Bog asphodel.

Heath bumblebee *(Bombus jonellus)*

The white back end of this bumblebee can often be spotted on heather heaths. Its size is between 9–14mm, and it resembles the garden bumblebee *(b. hortorum)* in that it has three yellow bands: one each at the front and back of the thorax and a third band at the top of the abdomen. However, the yellow of the heath bumblebee is more straw-coloured compared to the garden bumblebee. It also has a shorter face and the pollen baskets are pale, not black.

Common bird's foot trefoil *(Lotus corniculatus)* *(pysen-y-ceirw)*

This is very common flower on the periphery of the uplands flowering from May onwards. It prefers dry areas and can frequently be seen around quarry spoil. It is a low creeping plant and there can be up to eight of the bright yellow flowers on each stem. It is the seed pods which look like a bird's foot. The plant is poisonous as it contains hydrogen cyanide; it has, however, been used to stimulate respiration and improve digestion whilst also being thought of benefit in cancer treatment. An orange-yellow dye has been obtained from the flowers.

Bog asphodel *(Narthecium ossifragum)* *(llafn y bladur)*

As the name suggests, this is found in boggy areas. This is a true summer flower and will not be seen flowering before July, but its beautiful bright yellow star-like flowers will soon be dying out in August. It grows up to 15cm high and can be found in abundance in Cwm Idwal. It is easily recognised by its flattened sword-like leaves. Bog asphodel has been used as a yellow hair dye and as a substitute for saffron.

Cowberry *(Vaccinium vitis-idaea)* *(llusen goch)*

Oval shiny leaves differentiate this low creeping berry from the others. It is found in sheltered spots on mountain tops growing up to 15cm high; the Gallt yr Ogof area is particularly noteworthy. Although rather acidic, some people prefer them to cranberries (genuine wild cranberry can occasionally be found on boggy areas in North Wales). Cowberries are used by herbalists in the treatment of gonorrhoea, arthritis, rheumatism, diabetes and diarrhoea. The leaves can be used to make a yellow dye.

Cowberry.

Crowberry plant and (right) ripe crowberry.

Crowberry *(Empetrum nigrum)* *(creiglusen)*

An evergreen with shiny slim green leaves which form dense mats. The berries are initially pink then ripen to black, but are not as tasty as bilberries. A decoction of the roots has been used as eyewash to remove unwanted growths, but is probably safer used as a purple dye.

Devil's-bit scabious *(Succisa pratensis)* *(tamaid y cythraul)*

Found in damp grassy places, devil's-bit scabious is also a woodland indicator species. The plant can grow to nearly 1m high, but is usually shorter than this in the mountains. The flowers are up to 2cm in diameter. Generally useful to people, this plant has been known to provide all sorts of cures. It is for this reason that the plant has very short roots, the devil became angry and bit them off! The root was boiled down and drunk as a cure for the plague (scabious meaning itch) and poisons. Devil's-bit scabious has been used to ease eczema, reduce bruising and as a treatment for conjunctivitis. A green dye has been extracted from the leaves which can also be eaten in salads when young and fresh.

English stonecrop *(Sedum anglicum)* *(briweg y cerrig)*

Much to the frustration of a certain Welsh nature programme presenter, who I once had the pleasure of taking rock climbing, English stonecrop can be found all over North Wales. This is a very small plant which is no more than 5cm high. It is an early coloniser of scree slopes and is abundant anywhere there is scree or on quarry spoils. Often confused with the saxifrages, this delightful little flower has very distinctive succulent foliage which can be seen all year round. The flowers themselves arrive in June and can hang on until the end of August.

Devil's-bit scabious.

English stonecrop.

Golden rod *(Solidago virgaurea)* *(eurwialen)*

A rather scruffy looking plant, similar to ragweed but widely spread through woodlands and across heaths. In North Wales it makes regular appearances on cliff ledges growing between 15 and 60cm high, and flowers from July into October. A tea can be made from the leaves. Golden rod is considered a gentle remedy for many ailments such as cystitis, thrush and other urinary tract disorders. Its mild action has made it useful for treating children for gastro-enteritis. Mustard, orange and brown dyes have been obtained from the whole plant whilst a yellow dye has been extracted from the leaves and flowers.

Golden rod growing on the gully walls below Senior's Ridge in Cwm Idwal.

Gorse (and below).

Greater hawkbit on the ledges of Dinas Cromlech.

Gorse *(Ulex europaeus)* *(eithin Ffrengig)*

Dense, seemingly impregnable, clumps of gorse are a frequent sight on the grassy edges of the uplands. Very unpleasant to touch, the saving grace of gorse is its long-lasting flowers. Spring is the prime time but there seems to be some gorse in flower virtually all year round. In spring they have a gorgeous smell similar to coconut. The flowers are 2–3cm in size and reveal that gorse is a member of the pea family. Gorse bushes can grow to heights of between 2m and 3m. The spiky leaves are shed at no particular time of year and form a dense mat beneath the bush which prevents the growth of other plants. The flowers turn into black seedpods and, on a hot summer day, can be heard cracking open as the seeds are catapulted away from the parent bush. A sprig of gorse is said to prevent one from tumbling and will frighten away witches and fairies when hung over doorways. However, the good news is that kissing is in season when the gorse is in bloom! Gorse has been valuable as fuel in the past and was used by the Romans to filter silt in their gold mines. Gorse flowers can be pickled and used like capers in salads.

Greater hawkbit *(Leontodon hispidus)* *(peradyl garw)*

This common dandelion-like flower, also known as rough hawkbit, is widespread on grassland but can often be seen sprouting from crevices on Dinas Cromlech and around Cwm Idwal. It is usually round about 30cm tall. Its leaves, and indeed its flower, are very similar to that of the dandelion. The young leaves can be eaten raw or cooked but are not very nice! The roots have been used to make a coffee substitute. The plant is said to be useful in the treatment of kidney complaints and as a remedy for jaundice. The English name refers to an ancient belief that hawks ate these plants to sharpen their sight.

Harebell *(Campanula rotundifolia)* *(clychau'r eos)*

Harebells produce a very pretty and delicate flower, certainly one of my favourites. They were once devoured by sheep as soon as they appeared but with reduced sheep numbers on the hills today they can grow to 30cm or 40cm high. Their delicate pale blue flowers flutter gently on the mountain breeze. They tend to prefer dry grassland but will be seen along the footpath around Cwm Idwal in July, August and into September. An infusion of the roots has been used as curing drops for sore ears and a decoction of the plant has been drunk or used as a wash in the treatment of sore eyes.

Ling *(Calluna vulgaris)* *(grug)*

Also known as common heather, its tiny pink-purple flowers bring a riot of colour to the hills as summer progresses. Ling generally grows up to a height of 45cm but can be higher in mature stands. The shoots of this plant provide a tasty snack for foraging sheep, so it can often be seen growing on and around cliff faces or other places inaccessible to sheep. It is beginning to spread today as sheep numbers are reduced in some parts of the mountains. Although ling-covered slopes are probably more beautiful than the sight of heavily grazed grass slopes, if uncontrolled, ling (and indeed bell heather) can become very difficult to walk through; try skirting Moel Meirch above Llyn Gwynant on its east side! Ling has a long history of medicinal use. A tea can be made with the flowering stems and mead was once flavoured with its flowers. Brooms can be made by tying several twiggy branches together and we all know a small bunch in your car radiator grill will bring you good luck.

Common mouse-ear
(Cerastium fontanum) *(clust-y-llygoden gulddail)*

Found across Britain in grassy areas, this distinctive, pretty little flower can grow up to 30cm high on the mountains.

Harebells.

Ling (and inset)

Common mouse-ear.

Sneezewort.

St John's wort spotted growing next to the path in Cwm Idwal.

Selfheal.

Selfheal *(Prunella vulgaris)* *(y feddyges las)*

Selfheal grows in grassy areas, up to 18cm high, and is as its name suggests is thought to be a great healer. The leaves can be added to salads although they are a little bitter. A drink made from an infusion of the crushed leaves is said to be highly refreshing. Selfheal has a long history of being used as a treatment for wounds, ulcers and sores. Internally, it has been used to treat fever, diarrhoea and sore mouths. As if that weren't enough, the flowers and stems can be used to make an olive green dye.

Sneezewort *(Achillea ptarmica)* *(ystrewlys)*

This is another flower which has appeared in the meadows surrounding Cwm Idwal due to the reduction in sheep grazing. Flowering through July and August, the sneezewort lives in acidic, damp, grassy areas and will be between 30cm and 60cm high. One smell is said to be enough to make anyone sneeze, and if you hold its roots in your mouth the sharp taste is said to ease toothache.

St John's wort *(Hypericum perforatum)* *(eurinllys trydwll)*

Not a plant usually seen in the mountains, it is common in hedgerows and scrub areas in the south but quite localised in the north. Perhaps this plant is on the increase due to a reduction in sheep grazing. When the leaves are crushed they produce a red juice, which supposedly represents the blood of St John. The plant is known as *llysiau Ioan* in some parts of Wales, and was used to treat internal and external bruising. If a childless woman walks naked to pick this flower, she will conceive within the year! The St John's wort plants are very variable and it is difficult to say with complete certainty which species is which.

Snowdon lily *(Lloydia serotina)* *(lili'r Wyddfa)*

An icon of the National Park and one of its rarest plants. It grows in just five or six craggy locations inaccessible to both walkers and climbers. To see the Snowdon lily you will need rope access skills as well as well as a tip-off as to where they are flowering (each plant does not flower every season). The Snowdon lily inhabits the meadows of the European Alps and it is common in North America and Alaska where it is known as the common alp lily. It is a low growing plant, 7 to 10 cm high with narrow 'spidery' leaves, which flowers from late May or early June. Other Welsh names include *brwynddail y mynydd* (the rush-leaved mountain plant) and *y bryfedog* (the spiderwort). In Britain it is thought to be one of the first plants to be seriously threatened by global warming.

Snowdon lily.

Snowdonia hawkweed *(Hieracium snowdoniense)* *(heboglys eryri)*

One of the rarest plants in the world. In fact it has been thought extinct since 1955 but a single plant was discovered in Cwm Idwal in 2002. This hawkweed forms a rosette of gently toothed lance-shaped leaves which narrow towards the base to form a shaggy stalk. A slender stem bears a cluster of deep golden-yellow flower heads, not dissimilar to dandelions. It is a perennial plant that grows to about 30cm tall. The common hawkweed is a quite unremarkable plant and is very common; due to unusual reproductive biology it does lend itself to creating hundreds of very similar species.

Common valerian *(Valeriana officinalis)* *(llysiau Cadwgan)*

Commonly seen growing around the crags of Snowdonia, this unglamorous plant has adapted well to both wet and dry environments out of the reach of sheep. It can grow up to a metre tall but is usually smaller in the mountains. Look out also for red valerian (*Centranthus ruber* or *triaglog goch*) which is also common on cliffs and in disused quarries; it looks very much like common valerian but the flower is red. Commonly on sale today is valerian extract which is said to calm the nerves, allay pain and promote sleep.

Water mint *(Mentha aquatica)* *(mintys y dŵr)*

A common aromatic herb found in wet places, water mint grows up to 50cm high. It can be used as flavouring in cooked food or added raw to salads. It is, however, stronger than garden mint and as such is not popular. A tea made from the leaves has traditionally been used in the treatment of fevers, headaches, digestive disorders and various minor ailments. It has also been used as a mouthwash and a gargle for treating sore throats, ulcers and bad breath. The leaves are harvested as the plant comes into flower and can be dried for later use. The essential oil in the leaves is antiseptic; beware, it is toxic in large doses.

Hawkweed (and right).

Common valerian growing on Dinas Cromlech.

Water mint.

Welsh poppy.

Welsh poppy *(Meconopsis cambrica) (pabi Cymreig)*

Although not very common in the hills, the Welsh poppy can be seen by the path in the higher reaches of Cwm Idwal. It is abundant in local gardens and has become naturalised along the walls and roadside of the Nant Ffrancon. Cwm Idwal is one of the plant's highest altitude UK habitats. As with many other flowers, it suffers from sheep grazing. It grows to about 30cm high and usually nestles in rocky crevices. Plaid Cymru based their 2006 rebranded logo on the flower.

Western gorse *(Ulex gallii)* *(ethin mân)*

Western gorse is generally a lower growing plant than gorse. The flowers are smaller but its prickles are even more robust. As it name suggests, it is only found on the western margins of Britain so is quite common in North Wales. The colour is slightly less vivid than that of gorse and it will only grow on acid soils. However, free drainage is the most important factor governing where gorse grows. It flowers from August onwards.

Wild strawberry *(Fragaria vesca)* *(llwyn mefus mawr)*

This low hairy perennial is like a smaller version the garden strawberry. It grows through rooting runners in woodland, grassland and scrub environments. In North Wales it is abundant in the disused slate quarries and can often provided a tasty treat on belay ledges. The fruit is smaller than the garden strawberry so a lot would need to be picked to make jam. The berry is rich in iron and potassium and is thought to be excellent for sufferers of anaemia. The young leaves can be used in salads or dried and used to make a tea, which has been used as a treatment for diarrhoea. In India the root has been used to make a coffee substitute. A poultice made from the powdered leaves has been used to treat open sores.

Yellow pimpernel *(Lysimachia nemorum)* *(gwlyddyn melyn Mair)*

A small pretty yellow flower almost hidden in grassland. This plant prefers damp woodlands but can be seen in small numbers in the mountains. There is an excellent display in the woods at the bottom end of the Watkin Path. It flowers from May onwards and can grow up to 45cm tall when it needs to compete for light. Yellow pimpernel is an astringent herb which has been used to staunch bleeding.

Western gorse (and right).

Wild strawberry in the Dinorwig quarries.

Yellow pimpernel in Cwm Idwal.

Great woodrush.

Mat grass.

GRASSES & RUSHES

Grasses are difficult to identify, so here are a few of the more obvious and interesting types all easily recognisable when out on the hills.

Great woodrush *(Luzula sylvatica)* *(coedfrwynen fawr)*

Just one of many woodrush species, this one is common on the acid soils found in Snowdonia. It grows in clumps usually quite low in the hills. Its green, glossy leaves can grow taller than 1m. Clumps are found on dry well-drained ground where grazing is limited, and on cliff ledges where quite luxuriant clumps can grow together with other woodland-type plants.

Mat grass *(Nardus stricta)* *(cawnen ddu)*

The distinctive pale grass up to 1m tall forming dense tufts, but usually shorter, which always looks dry. It covers large areas of the grassy parts of the hills. Through the season it becomes hard and fibrous enough to deter sheep; small clumps will often been seen strewn around having been picked by the sheep then discarded in favour of tastier grasses. Sheep are selective about what they eat and will only touch mat grass in the spring, leaving it to dominate other grass species over wide areas of the National Park. The large swathes of mat grass on Snowdonia's drier slopes indicate unsustainably heavy grazing. Mat grass-dominated hillsides support fewer plant species than areas of more natural vegetation.

Purple moor grass *(Molinia caerulea)* **(glaswellt y gweunydd)**

A reddish-coloured grass, this is a very good indicator of boggy ground. It can grow up to 1m high but is usually lower in the uplands. Green when young, it turns a reddish colour when mature. The seed heads are usually dark purple and flower from June until September. Like mat grass, *Molinia* is unpalatable to sheep after the first flush of growth in spring. Where levels of sheep grazing are high, it can dominate on wetter ground as sheep avoid it and graze more palatable grasses. It can be difficult to reduce this dominance and restore the diversity of plants. One of the best ways is to graze the land with cattle, less selective grazers than sheep. Being heavier animals, they trample the ground and break up the tussocks allowing other species to germinate and grow.

Soft-rush *(Juncus effusus)* **(brwynen babwyr)**

Quite common and very distinctive, soft-rush grows in clumps up to just over 1m high usually in damp places. Very unpalatable, untouched by sheep and is probably toxic to mammals. It has, however, been used to treat sore throats, jaundice, acute urinary tract infection and the morbid crying of babies. Soft-rush has been much more useful as a weaving material, however. A cheap candle used to be made from soft-rush; the stem was peeled then soaked in the dripping fat from cooking meat. When burned, this gave a yellow, smoky and rather dim light. This was once a common practice in rural areas. When more light was required, the wick would be folded in half and burnt at both ends at the same time. It's thought that this is where the expression 'burning the candle at both ends' come from.

Purple moor grass (and below).

Soft-rush (and left).

Birch.

White birch bark and leaves.
© iStockphoto.com

Fly agaric often grows under birch trees.

TREES & SHRUBS

Birch *(Betula pubescens)* **(bedwen lwyd)**

The downy birch is also known as white birch or hairy birch. As the Ice Age drew to a close, birch trees were among the first to drift northwards and colonise the British Isles. As the climate continued to improve, oak become the dominant species in the lower areas while birch retreated to the poorer soils and wetter areas in the north and the west. The birch woodlands of North West Scotland provide a rich ecosystem which features a wide range of fauna and flora; this can be seen on a smaller scale in Wales. There are 140 species of moth which can live on birch. Birch areas can be rich in edible fungi; however, one which should not be eaten is the easily recognisable fly agaric.

Birch wood is very tough and durable. It is also waterproof and as such can be used to make drinking vessels, canoe skins and roofing tiles, etc. To make canoe skins the outer bark is carefully removed then pressed flat and stored. When required, it would be heated over a fire to make it pliable for shaping to the canoe frame. The birch tree is associated with many medicinal uses. An infusion of the leaves can be used to treat gout, dropsy and rheumatism, and it is recommended as a reliable solvent of kidney stones. Food and drink-wise, the birch is most famous for its sweet sap which can be tapped off carefully to make wine or beer or even drunk neat.

Bog myrtle (and left).

Bog myrtle *(Myrica gale) (gwyrddling)*

This fragrant shrub, also known as sweet gale, colonizes damp areas and can grow to over 1m tall. It is remarkable in that it is one of the very few British plant species which can change sex from year to year. It has also been noticed that midges do not frequent areas where bog myrtle grows and British companies are currently investigating how bog myrtle affects midges to produce a repellant. Bog myrtle has been used to improve the flavour of beer and to increase foaming. A wax covering on the fruit and leaves can be extracted by scalding the fruit with boiling water. This wax can be used to make aromatic candles; unfortunately, the amount of wax collected is tiny. An Irish legend tells that it was the wood from the bog mrytle which was used to make the cross upon which Jesus was crucified; the plant has subsequently been too embarrassed to grow any taller!

Dwarf willow *(Salix herbacea) (helygen fach)*

This tiny member of the willow family is a true arctic-alpine species rarely found below 600m in the UK. In Snowdonia it can be observed on the summit of Y Garn and in some parts of the Carneddau, where it grows in shallow stony soils exposed to the full force of the wind. It is one of the smallest woody plants in the world growing between one and six centimetres tall. It has rounded well-veined leaves which are 1-2cm long and broad. In Wales its distribution is carefully monitored to see how it is fairing as our climate warms. In the photograph we can see what look like red berries. In fact they are insect galls of an arctic species of sawfly which can only breed on *Salix herbacea*. It is also known as least willow.

Dwarf willow.

Hawthorn tree, (left) leaves and (inset) May blossom.

Hawthorn *(Crataegus monogyna)* *(draenen wen)*

This deciduous and easily recognisable tree grows in abundance on our uplands. The young shoots are very attractive to sheep but, once established, the strong thorns make them particularly unpalatable. Many Snowdonia hillsides are dotted with hawthorns which established themselves during the Great Depression of the 1930s when sheep were less abundant on the hills. Hawthorn leaves, when young, can be eaten in salads. The tough heavy wood has been used over the years to make excellent walking sticks and tool handles and it is also extremely good firewood. The berries, or haws, are very attractive to birds and the blossom has been used in sweet puddings. The hawthorn is considered a very valuable medicinal herb. It is used by western herbalists as 'food for the heart' and is thought to be good for treating disorders of the heart and circulation system, especially angina.

Goat willow *(Salix caprea) (helygen ddeilgron)*

Goat willow will often be seen lining the banks of fast flowing streams and along lakesides in Snowdonia. There are many different types of willows; all have some form of catkin as their seed but goat willow is the most abundant here. It is often a multi branched dense shrubby tree rather like a large bush rarely reaching more than 12m tall. Catkins usually appear before the leaves are open. The male catkins are bright yellow whilst the female ones are rather more greyish; the two are to be found on separate trees often with some considerable distance between them. The goat willow is sometimes known as pussy willow as the silky grey buds from which the catkins appear resemble cats' paws. The willow is home to a great many insects, particularly for the larvae of moths, indeed the purple emperor butterfly will feed on nothing else. Although cricket bats are famously made from willow they are made from the white willow which also is known as the cricket bat willow. The goat willow does not produce useful timber as it tends to be quite brittle and is know to crack rather violently when burned. Tanin and salicin (an anti-inflammatory) can be extracted from the bark.

Goat willow (and inset).

Holly *(Ilex aquifolium) (celynnen)*

Everyone recognises holly from its wide use as a decoration at Christmas. In fact, in pre-Victorian times, it was known as the Christmas tree. Holly had significance in folklore long before it came to represent the crown of thorns worn by Jesus. A pre-Christian celebration demanded that a boy be dressed in a suit of holly leaves and a girl similarly in ivy. They would then parade around the village, bringing nature through the darkest part of the year to re-emerge for another year's fertility. Holly trees were traditionally known for protection against lightning strikes, which led to them being frequently planted near houses. We now know that the spines on the prickly holly leaves can act as miniature lightning conductors, protecting the tree and other nearby objects. Holly is an evergreen hard wood which grows well in the unhelpful climate of Snowdonia's mountains. The bright red berries are an important source of food for birds, but are poisonous to humans. The creamy-white wood makes a good wood for carving and burns very well. Notice the way the leaves are less spiky the higher up the tree they are.

Holly. (Top right) spikeless upper leaves. (Right) ripening berries.

Juniper *(Juniperus communis)* *(merywen)*

Juniper on the mountains, a low, trailing woody plant found in random spots over the mountains of North Wales, differs from the juniper trees found on the chalk downlands of England, where it grows upright to about 4m high. A particularly good location is on the south-east side of Lliwedd. It is the same species, but has simply adapted to life in the harsh mountains. Its berries can still be used to flavour gin and game. Although its wood is very good for producing charcoal and pencils, it is illegal to harvest it. The Romans recognised the value of juniper and used the berries to cure stomach ailments. The famous mediaeval herbalist Culpepper recommended juniper berries for a wide variety of conditions including the treatment of flatulence, for which juniper oil is still used today. Juniper has the largest geographic range of any woody plant in the world; however its appearance in Wales is minimal and it is now the subject of a Biodiversity Action Plan. Walkers and climbers are asked to report their sightings of Juniper by completing a survey form at www. plantlife.org.uk/juniper.

Juniper (and right).

© iStockphoto.com

Sessile oak *(Quercus petraea)* *(derwen mes di-goes)*

There are over 500 species in the northern hemisphere but only two species of oak are indiginous to the British Isles; of these the sessile oak with its domed shape is the most common in Snowdonia. It is a little squatter than the pedunculate or English oak, the indentations on the leaves are less pronounced and its acorns are more rounded. Oak wood is much sought after and, were the wood not so good for building and ship making, there might be a great deal more ancient oak forest left. The oak is prevalent in the mythology of many civilisations; one local story involves the Welsh goddess Arianrhod who forbade her son, Lleu Llaw Gyffes to marry a mortal. Lleu's uncles Gwydion and Math created a beautiful woman called Blodeuwedd from Flowers and Oak. Unfortunately while Lleu was away Blodeuwedd fell in love with another man. Lleu killed that man and his uncle Gwydion turned Blodeuwedd into an Owl as punishment, that her face should never again see the light of day.

When making plans for the summer, watch for when the oak and ash come into leaf in the spring:

> *If the oak before the ash,*
> *Then we'll only have a splash.*
> *If the ash before the oak,*
> *Then we'll surely have a soak!*

Rowan *(Sorbus aucuparia)* **(cerddinen** or *criafolen)*

The rowan, also known as mountain ash or witch wood, is another very distinctive tree of the Welsh uplands. In fact, it can grow at higher altitudes than any other native broadleaved tree. Often found growing close to old ruins, this tree has been revered for many years due to its magical properties. In Wales, it was planted in churchyards to keep the dead in their graves and ward off ghosts. A sprig was frequently placed above the entrance to animal houses to keep witches and other demons at bay. The Latin name translates as 'fowler's service tree' and this relates to the use of the berries as bait by bird trappers in mediaeval times. In parts of Wales, the berries have been used to produce strong intoxicating ale. Although the fruit is very acidic, it has been used to make jam. This jam is also thought, by herbalists, to be good for treating diarrhoea, haemorrhoids and vaginal discharge. A black dye has been made from the tree and it is also considered excellent for turning into barrels, cogs and furniture.

Silver birch *(Betula pendula)* **(bedwen arian)*

The silver birch is easily recognised by its fragile silvery bark which can be used as kindling. It prefers drier areas than the downy birch, and is a good early coloniser of scree slopes where the soil is thin. As such, it loves the large areas of slate waste found in Snowdonia, and can be found colonising the Dinorwig slate quarries in profusion.

Peat *(mawn)*

The woody heritage of peat can readily be seen on the mountains. There are places where remnant tree stumps are visible in the peat, demonstrating that Snowdonia was once tree covered to a greater extent than today. The pre-agricultural, pre-historic landscape would have been thick deciduous forest, the tree-line broken only by the most exposed and weather-beaten peaks.

Rowen. (Right) leaves
and (inset) berries.

Silver birch on slate waste.
Silver birch bark and leaf (right).

Peat at the northern end of the
Moelwynion above Pen y Gwryd.

Bracken.

Hard fern.

FERNS

Bracken *(Pteridium aquilinum)* *(rhedynen ungoes)*

Bracken is the fern that everyone can recognise; it's everywhere and it's spreading. Its fronds grow up to 180cm tall. Originally a woodland plant, it spread prolifically across hillsides in the 20th century, due in part to the focus on sheep grazing and the decline of traditional uses, including harvesting for animal bedding. Sheep have no interest in it, so it can spread and flourish where sheep farming is dominant. There are some effective herbicides available, but it spreads by way of an underground rhizome which is difficult to restrain. One of the best ways of limiting its growth is the introduction of cattle who will trample it flat (one reason why there are more cattle on the hills today).

Bracken can harbour the sheep ticks that pass Lyme disease to humans and it is poisonous to cattle, horses, sheep and people. Although bracken leaves have been shown to be carcinogenic, the plant has been put to many remarkable uses. The roots have been ground and made into dumplings, the curled up young fronds (fiddleheads) are considered a delicacy in Japan and in some areas of the US and Canada (they have to be carefully prepared so don't try this at home) and the rhizomes can be used as soap! There is currently some interest in harvesting bracken to make compost.

Hard fern *(Blechnum spicant)* **(gwibredynen)**

This is one of the more common ferns. It likes to be in shady places and is often found in rock crevices, growing to a height of 10–75cm tall. The fertile fronds will stand erect and remain evergreen while the sterile fronds are low-lying and die off in the winter. It has been used as an emergency food source and it is said that chewing the leaves will alleviate thirst. However, since most ferns are carcinogenic, better to risk the stream water!

Maidenhair spleenwort

(Asplenium trichomanes) **(duegredynen gwallt y forwyn)**

This is a very pretty little fern and will be seen adorning walls over Snowdonia, growing to a height of 5–15cm tall. There are particularly good displays in the derelict buildings alongside the Watkin and Miner's paths up Snowdon. The dried fronds can be used to make a tea which is good for chest complaints and to promote menstruation.

Male fern *(Dryopteris filix-mas)* **(marchredynen gyffredin)**

This fern grows in large shuttlecock-shaped clumps and is very common in woodlands, growing to heights of 40–90cm. It likes shady wet spots and is often found near ruins and in old quarries in the mountains. Tin Can Alley (a disused hone-stone quarry) just behind Idwal Cottage is a good place to look. Its spores bestow invisibility on their carrier and its roots were used to ward off evil spirits by being shaped like a hand and baked. A popular, and apparently effective, treatment for tapeworm can be made from the roots.

Parsley fern *(Cryptogramma crispa)* **(rhedynen bersli)**

A very pretty little fern which is an early coloniser of scree slopes. It is restricted to well-drained acid rocks and can be seen all over Snowdonia's mountains. There are particularly good displays in the Dinorwig slate quarries, growing up to 30cm tall. It has upright fertile leaves growing above the sterile lower fronds. Generally distributed over the north-west of the UK, it is common in the Lake District and western Scotland where is has been recorded at a height of 1280m (Ben Nevis). It has no known culinary uses and its name comes from being a look-a-like rather than a taste-a-like!

Rusty back *(Ceterach officinarum)* *(duegredynen gefngoch)*

A distinctive fern often seen on stone walls and in rocky areas. The underside is characteristically covered in rusty brown scales. The fronds are divided into rounded lobes and can be up to 20cm long.

Maidenhair spleenwort.

Male fern.

Parsley fern.

Rusty back fern in the Dinorwig Quarries.

Himalayan balsam growing below Llyn Lockwood by Pen y Gwryd. (Inset) a close-up.

New Zealand willowherb (left) and (below) its tiny flowers.

INVADERS

As well as the many native flowers and ferns, many non-native plants and species not normally found on upland have become established.

Himalayan balsam *(Impatiens glandulifera)* **(ffromlys chwarennog)**
This tall annual plant was introduced to Kew Gardens in 1839 as a garden plant. It escaped to the wild and has become naturalised right across the British Isles. It grows up to 2m tall and has become a characteristic riverbank species. The dense stands suffocate other plants, so when it dies away in the winter riverbanks are left bare and susceptible to erosion. The flowers vary from pale pink to purple and appear from June to October. Their shape resembles a policeman's helmet, one of its common names. Other names include Indian touch-me-not, ornamental jewelweed, pink peril and poor man's orchid. They produce copious amounts of nectar and draw pollinating insects away from native plants. A single plant can set about 800 seeds. The seed capsules react to the slightest disturbance, causing it to split along its length then curl up and twist explosively, projecting the contents up to 7m away. The black, spherical seeds are about 2–3mm across and remain viable for about two years, requiring cold for germination in February or March. They are buoyant and can travel along waterways to infest new areas, even germinating underwater. The stems can be eaten after boiling and a yellow dye can be extracted from the whole plant.

New Zealand willowherb

(Epilobium brunnescens) **(helyglys gorweddol)**

This is a very low-growing plant with almost circular short-stalked leaves attached to stems which root as they creep over the ground. The foliage becomes orangey-brown as the plant matures. It arrived accidentally from its native New Zealand in 1908. It is usually found on paths and in crevices in walls. It likes alpine conditions, so is now widespread. The delicate pinkish-white flowers are held aloft on long ovaries and are similar to those of mouse-ear. The seed capsules split into three when they mature, curling backwards to release the seeds.

Rhododendron *(Rhododendron ponticum)* **(rhododendron wyllt)**

The rhododendron is native to countries in the western and eastern Mediterranean such as Spain, Portugal and Turkey, and also occurs in Asia. It was first introduced to Britain in the late 18th century. It became especially popular on country estates in Victorian times, providing ornamental value as well as cover for game birds. It can now be seen spreading out from gardens onto the hills and is particularly rife in the Moelwynion. The plant is responsible for the destruction of many native habitats, as it will out-compete most native plants. Very little light penetrates its thick leaf canopy, which prevents the germination of other competing native plants. This in turn leads to the consequent loss of the associated native animals. The rhododendron thrives in milder, wet conditions, where there are poor, acidic soils. It invades areas both vegetatively and via seed. Established plants spread by horizontal growth of branches. A single plant may eventually end up covering many metres of ground with thickly interlaced, impenetrable branches. Where the horizontal branches touch the ground they will root, continually extending the area of cover.

It is worth noting that because of its extremely lateral growth form, rhododendron plants are capable of extending into areas which otherwise would not be hospitable to them. For example, it is capable of dominating large areas of wetland with its canopy, while the main stem and roots of the plant are well back on suitably dry land.

Rhododendron seeds are tiny and are dispersed by the wind. Each flower head can produce 3,000–7,000 seeds, so that a large bush can produce several million seeds per year. Not all the seeds will grow successfully, but given the right conditions a good many will germinate.

Seedlings have difficulty becoming established in areas where there is already continuous ground cover from native plants. They are more likely to succeed in freshly disturbed soil. The seedlings also germinate well in moss covered areas, perhaps because of the water-holding capacity of the mosses.

Grazing animals are discouraged from eating rhododendron by its tough unpalatable leaves. Inexperienced or extremely hungry sheep and cattle occasionally eat enough to be poisoned. This toxicity of rhododendron to herbivores means that it cannot be controlled by grazing.

Cases of human poisoning are also known; in particular the consumption of honey produced from rhododendron flowers, known as 'mad honey disease' or 'honey intoxication'. Cases of this have been recorded from as far back as 400 BC. It results in relatively short-lived intestinal and cardiac problems and is rarely fatal.

Rhododendron growing amongst heather high on the Moelwynnion and (inset) flowers.

AUTUMN

Toadstools on dung.

Birch polypore.

FUNGI

Autumn is the prime time of year for fungi. The grassy areas of our uplands contain many fungi known to experts as LBJs (little brown jobs); identifying them involves all sorts of specialised techniques. Here are just a few of the fungi you are most likely to see on the hill or when leaving the wooded areas. Of particular note are the splendid toadstools and mushrooms which grow in the cow dung around the base of Tryfan, in Cwm Idwal and in Cwm y Llan.

Sheep dung yields a few small specimens and there are also some to be found in bogs and on the grassland. Wherever there are trees, there will be some fungi to inspect. Fungi always grows on organic matter be it dung, wood or other rotting vegetation.

There are many thousands of fungi in the British Isles and most fungi identification books only contain the most common hundred or so from a range of habitats. Identification can be very difficult so if determined to eat the fungi found, referring to a fungi expert is strongly recommended! To identify fungi, it is best to take them home in a dry container and take note of all the different aspects of the fungi such as cap shape, gill, stem, habitat and colour. Common names can be regional and mycologists insist we use the Latin names to avoid confusion. Most fungi vary their shape and colour as they mature, making identification even more difficult.

Birch polypore *(Piptoporus betulinus)*

This common bracket fungus is found, as the name suggests, on birch trees. Usually on the trunk of dead or dying trees, it attacks the heartwood and sapwood. The very firm flesh has been used for sharpening razors and this gives rise to the alternative name of razor-strop fungus. The brackets can be between 10cm and 20cm across and 3–8cm thick. It begins life in a rounded form maturing into a hoof shape. The underside and rim is white and the convex top turns pale brown. It can be found all year round and although technically edible, it has an acquired taste!

Boletes, recognisable by its lack of gills.

Boletes

Boletes are characterized by their lack of gills. Instead, they have tubes which open through pores, giving a sponge-like appearance under the cap. Some of the boletes can grow to 30cm across, so will stand out boldly as you pass through the broad-leaved woodlands on your way to the open land above. Most, but not all, of the boletes provide good eating.

Butter waxcap *(Hygrocybe ceracea)*

This small yellow agaric is found in sheep-cropped grass, usually in small groups. It has a greasy cap and a dry stem, sometimes with an orange tinge. The cap becomes flatter and depressed as it matures. The cap will be between 1cm and 4cm across and the stem may be 2–4cm tall. The butter waxcap is edible.

Butter waxcap (and right).

Common jelly spot.

Fly agaric in the woods at Fachwen, a popular spot for novice rock climbers.

Common jelly spot *(Dacrymyces stillatus)*

The common jelly spot is a frequently occurring fungus. It is found on rotting wood of all kinds in damp places. The small, never more than 5mm, cushion-like fruiting bodies are crowded together and sometime merge. The flesh is soft yet firm and it can be seen all year round but is most obvious in the autumn. It is inedible.

Fly agaric *(Amanita muscaria)*

The fly agaric is a large fleshy and easily-recognised fungi. Look for a bulbous base, white patches on a bright red cap and white gills. The fly agaric grows on poor sandy soils favouring birch wood but also pines. It can be found in many of the woody areas peripheral to the mountains.

Hygrocybe helobia
(and right).

Hygrocybe helobia

This is a small agaric with a reddish-orange cap about 1–3cm in diameter. The stem is between 2cm and 4cm tall. It grows in sheep-cropped grass, moss and generally poor pasture land. The youthful cap is convex and becomes more flattened with maturity. Helobia is found in small groups from late summer to late autumn, is not terribly common and is inedible.

Jelly-antler fungus *(Calocera viscosa)*

This is a very common bright yellow fungus, which can vary slightly in appearance with the fruiting body being either branched or forked. It has a sticky but firm and pliable texture. The jelly-antler fungus can be spotted growing from the end of summer right into the early winter and will be seen on rotting tree stumps or sawn off telegraph poles. It is usually between 2cm and 8cm tall.

Jelly-antler fungus.

Jew's ear *(Auricularia auricula-judae)*

This spectacular purple-brown fungus is seen growing on the branches of living and dying broad-leaved trees, such as elder. It can often be seen around abandoned settlements and will grow to up to 8cm in diameter. It can spread to cover large areas of the underside of branches, away from direct sunlight. The name is actually a corruption of Judas's ear after Judas Iscariot who, it is said, hanged himself on an elder tree after his betrayal of Jesus Christ.

Liberty cap *(Psilocybe semilanceata)*

The liberty cap is a notorious little mushroom, known by some as the 'magic' mushroom. It contains the hallucinatory drug psilocybin. The liberty cap grows in areas of sheep-cropped grass and has a distinctive though not unique pointed bell-shaped cap which is 5–20mm across. The tall slender stem, reaching a height of 10cm, is quite characteristic. It can be found from late summer into the autumn and is legally a Class A drug.

Jew's ear.

Liberty cap.

Milk bonnet *(Mycena galopus)*

This grows in small groups in mixed woods and on old fire sites. Galopus can reach a height of 5–10cm tall with a cap 1–2cm across. It is a dark brownish-grey colour, although some of the other galopus are pure white. It is most definitely inedible and should have a faint smell of radish. If broken, it will extrude white milky droplets from the stem. This 'milk' gives rise to names such as the milk cap or milk bonnet.

Scarlet caterpillar fungus *(Cordyceps militaris)*

This cheesy wotsit look-a-like was spotted growing in the short sheep-cropped grass just behind Jerry's Roof in the Llanberis Pass. The scarlet caterpillar fungus is remarkable and quite rare. The reddish-orange elongated fruiting body grows to nearly 5cm long. Although all fungi grow on organic matter such as wood, leaf mulch or dung, the scarlet caterpillar fungus grows from the pupa of a moth or butterfly found just under the ground. The fungus eats the pupa: a truly parasitic fungus.

Shaggy ink cap *(Coprinus comatus)*

Coprinus comatus, also known as judge's wig or lawyer's wig, is an edible species which pops up on lawns and in roadside verges in late summer and the autumn. It is quite distinctive and not easily confused with other species. Seen here in its freshly appeared white form this fungus soon blackens and turns into an inky fluid. The young ink caps are the best for eating, try get them before they open out (and have their identity confirmed by a fungi expert). If you are brave you can bake them with eggs or create a shaggy cup ketchup.

Shiny hay cap *(Panaeolus semiovatus)*

A large and proud specimen, it stands tall in the cow dung in Snowdonia's northern mountains. The shiny hay cap can be up to 15cm tall with a cap of 5cm across. The cap is shiny when dry, hence the common name. Look out for the ring on the stem as a key to identification and the mottled gills which turn dark brown. The black edging in the photograph consists of the spores. Given its habitat, it is inedible and very unappetising!

Milk bonnet (and right).

Scarlet caterpillar fungus.

Shaggy ink caps on the lawn at Plas y Brenin.

Shiny hay cap.

Snowy waxcap (and right).

Snowy waxcap *(Hygrocybe virginea)*

This is a white, greasy agaric found in acidic areas of sheep-cropped grass and sometimes in open woodland. The cap is 1–3cm across and the stem is 2–5cm tall. Pure white when young, the *virginea* tinges ivory with age. It can be found from late summer into the autumn and is quite common. It is inedible.

Splendid waxcap *(Hygrocybe splendidissima)*

The splendid waxcap is a very distinctive red toadstool. There are some similar species with which confusion is possible; note than none of them are edible. They can be found in short cropped grass and will often sprout up in places sheep have been grazing. They have a greasy cap and pale yellow gills. They can grow up to 6cm tall with a diameter of up to 4cm.

Splendid waxcap (and right).

Unknown yellow

I couldn't resist adding this fine little yellow toadstool. It was found growing in a very damp acidic bog in Cwm Clogwyn on Snowdon. It is obviously
a young specimen and this makes it very difficult to identify. It might be
another *Hygrocybe*.

We have trawled through our fungi resources and even our friendly expert
has failed to name it. Maybe you can?

Yellowing cup *(Peziza succosa)*

There are many species in the genus *Peziza*. They all have a similar form
but will be found growing in a range of habitats from woodland floors and
manure to masonry and bonfire sites. The yellowing cup grows in mixed
woodland and favours path-side locations. Look for large, up to 10cm in
diameter, smooth brown rubber-like growth. If the flesh is broken, a watery
juice seeps out and turns yellow on contact with the air. It is poisonous.

Yellowleg bonnet *(Mycena epipterygia)*

Mycena are a species of generally delicate toadstools often found in
broadleaved woods. Although there are several variations in the family,
the almost translucent stem is a good indicator of *Mycena epipterygia*. It
grows up to 8cm tall with a cap of up to 2cm diameter. *M. epipterygia* has
a bell-shaped cap which is generally yellowish brown. It is found in small
groups in mossy or grassy damp places.

Unknown yellow,
in damp bog.

Yellowing cup.

Yellowleg bonnet.

Stone circle on the northern Carneddau.

Trees growing on cliff faces out of reach of sheep.

HILL FARMS

There is no landscape in Britain (apart from a few small coastal margins) that is untouched by the actions of people; Snowdonia is no exception. Large areas of the national park exhibit the scars of slate quarrying and mineral mining. Today the hills and mountains are criss-crossed by paths created by today's leisure users and the valleys are dominated by roads and settlements. Although the agricultural impact on Britain's lowlands is glaringly obvious, it is by no means absent from the uplands.

Two thousand years ago, most of the valley sides, up to a height of around 700m, were covered in trees. Iron Age people lived on the top of the Carneddau as the valleys were very inhospitable and lacked the defensive protection that hilltops offered.

Today, flowers such as bluebells and wood sorrel can be found growing on the high ground. These flowers are remnants of that once vast woodland. Many of the craggy areas on the mountains have a few trees growing just out of reach of the sheep, such as holly and rowan.

Goats

Most of the woodland has been cleared for grazing animals which limits regeneration of the woodlands on the high ground. Sheep are the major commodity, although goat farming has also been tried but proved to be uneconomical. The goats we see on the hill today are remnants of flocks from when Cistercian monks managed much of the land in mediaeval times. Goats were reputedly kept in conjunction with cattle, with the goats being used to graze the steeper slopes and cliff tops to discourage cattle from venturing onto those areas. The low walls (so-called 'cattle walls') above many cliffs, such as on top of Tryfan Bach or Carreg Wastad, would have been built to prevent cattle from being enticed onto the steeper ground by nutrient-rich vegetation. Beyond the clearance of woodland, the legacy of farming on our hills includes dry stone walls and ruined buildings.

Government subsidy

Agriculture remains important in Snowdonia, employing a significant number of people. However, the poor quality of grazing and competition from lowland farmers makes it difficult to remain economically viable. Farming still has a major influence on the upland landscape. Today's farmers receive public money to maintain the character of the landscape and in some cases improve it, rather than the previous system of subsidy per head of stock.

The web of dry stone walls stretches all across Snowdonia, some in improbable places.

Tal y Llyn farm, Ogwen Valley.

Summer & winter farms

During the 18th century, farmers would drive their animals from the lowlands to summer grazing on the hillsides. Shepherds would live on the mountain, sometimes taking their whole families to summer farms *(hafod)* before returning to their winter farm *(hendre)*. These names are still commonplace across our maps. While living in the hafod, the families would cut grass (including bog grass) for hay. The small square ruins we come across on the hill are often old hay barns and not sheepfolds as often labelled on Ordnance Survey maps.

Sheep

In the latter part of the 20th century, the number of sheep on the hill increased significantly. Sheep eat continuously, but selectively, and their presence has led to localised overgrazing. This has exacerbated the effect of walkers' feet, by leaving a thin plant cover which is easily worn away. Overgrazing damages both the quantity and quality of the natural grassland, reducing diversity and encouraging the growth of blanket areas of coarse unpalatable grasses such as mat grass. This is a particular problem on the summit ridges where vegetation is fragile. Heather and gorse can take over where sheep grazing is reduced, making large areas of the hill difficult and unpleasant to walk, so flock sizes of sustainable numbers are important.

On land owned by the National Trust, tenants are encouraged not to graze sheep on the high mountains during the winter months. Grass does not grow in the winter, so if the sheep eat all the winter grass there will be less for the spring lambs. When grass growth is low or non-existent in winter, sheep will graze on young heather, which inhibits its growth too.

The result of experiments in fencing off areas to keep sheep out can be seen in some places, notably in Cwm Idwal. The vegetation there is quite different to the usual grass mix found elsewhere. However, walking through the waist-deep heather on the eastern side of Moel Meirch in the Moelwynion, where there has been very little grazing, is quite unpleasant.

The sheep farmer's year

The farmer's year has remained unchanged for many years. Pregnant ewes are kept on the lower land during the winter (some hill farmers own or rent land on the sunny isle of Anglesey). Lambing begins in March and is usually completed by April when the ewes are sorted by the number of lambs they have. The ewes will also be vaccinated and have their hooves trimmed to minimise foot rot. Lambing is a busy and stressful time of year for the sheep farmers; while subsidies keep the farms going, it is the annual production of lambs which provide any profit. The lambs are vulnerable to foxes, crows and even, it has been reported on the Lleyn, to herring gulls. Initially ewes and lambs are turned onto the *fridd*, the semi-enclosed areas between the enclosed low-land and the mountain wall. Barren ewes and yearlings (the previous year's female lambs) are turned out onto the open mountain to re-establish the *cynefin* or heft (a sheep's territory). Each ewe will return to the same patch of hillside year after year. In May, the male lambs are castrated, and all the lambs are ear-notched and tagged then sent back onto the mountainside with their mothers.

The sheep are brought down off the hill in June for shearing and to vaccinate the lambs. September sees the big round-up of the mountain flocks as this is when the lambs of that year are brought down to be prepared for market. It is a fantastic sight to see the sheep dogs covering miles of steep mountainside to gather in the sheep. Each dog will be guided by the harsh call of the shepherds (sadly, the only time of year when the Welsh language is prolific across the mountainsides of Snowdonia). In October, the ewes will be dipped and have the wool around their tails clipped in preparation for tupping (mating). During the winter, the sheep are provided with food supplements in a solid form; these sheep licks are often seen on the hill in late autumn and the winter.

Sheep on the hillside.

Sheep lick.

Bringing sheep down off the hill in the Llanberis Pass.

Welsh Black cattle in Cwm y Llan on Snowdon.

Mat grass pulled up and rejected by grazing sheep.

Cattle

Recent years have seen a return to the hills of the Welsh Black cattle. The National Trust and other conservation bodies have been very keen to re-introduce cattle to the farms they own. Cattle graze differently to sheep: they are less selective, have larger mouths, graze over a wider area and cannot graze as close to the ground as sheep. Sheep are notorious patch grazers, tending to stay in one place and nibble the best grass right down to its roots as well as any other tasty morsels such as young bilberry and heather shoots. This leaves large areas of less tasty grass, such as matt grass, to flourish. Cattle also trample bracken and are probably the only effective method of controlling its spread. Spraying does not kill the whole plant as it can spread through underground shoots known as rhizomes. The Welsh Black also produces excellent meat, made available in the local butchers' shops providing a welcome extra income for the hill farmers. The Welsh Black is a hardy breed; it can stay out on the hill most of the year and does an excellent job of converting rough pasture into top quality beef.

Y Meini Hirion.

Llyn Idwal.

MYTHS & LEGENDS

Y Tylwyth Teg

Y Tylwyth Teg are the fairies of Wales. Some are good, some are bad. They can be small enough to hide in the petals of flowers or large enough to pass as mortals. Y Tylwyth Teg live in an underground kingdom and visit our world through lakes, ponds and submerged caves. They love to dance on moonlight nights and misty days in energetic circles. The womenfolk are very beautiful and will, from time to time, entice mortal men into the dance. The men will be trapped in the dance for a year and a day and can only be rescued by a branch of rowan held out to them, for rowan is repellent to Y Tylwyth Teg. The men will not believe how long they have been dancing. To them, it will seem a matter of minutes and they will not be tired, hungry or thirsty. They will only believe how long they have been absent when they are shown the wear on their shoes.

Y Meini Hirion – the good and the bad

On the far northern end of the Carneddau lies upland Snowdonia's only significant ancient monument, erroneously known as the Druid's Circle. The cremated remains of a young child were discovered in the centre of the circle in the 1960s. There are two stones which are larger than the others and have special importance. The Deity Stone will lean over and hit whoever swears in its vicinity and will bellow out a warning to any witches involved in morbid rituals. The Stone of Sacrifice has a small hollow in it. If a baby is placed there before it is a month old, it will enjoy good fortune for the rest of its life.

Llyn Idwal

In the 12th century, Owain ap Gwynedd (Prince of Gwynedd) had a young son called Idwal. Idwal was not a fighting man but was an excellent scholar, so when Owain had to leave the area to go to battle he left Idwal in the care of his cousin Nefydd.

Unfortunately, Nefydd's son Dunawt was not the brightest, and the arrival of Idwal showed him up. Nefydd was jealous that Owain should have such a bright and likeable boy of sparkling humour and intellect, constantly overshadowing his own son Dunawt. One morning, Nefydd suggested that Dunawt take Idwal for a walk around the lake and push Idwal in when he got the opportunity. They both knew Idwal could not swim. As the two boys set off, the sun shone brightly and Idwal, uplifted by his environs, sung merrily. As they reached a point where the lake dropped deeply from the shore, Dunawt gave Idwal a mighty push. Idwal tumbled into the water and shouted for help as he struggled to stay above the surface. His efforts were in vain, however, as Dunawt laughed down upon him.

Owain was distraught at the death of his son and suspected Nefydd and Dunawt of foul play. He banished them from the kingdom and named the lake Llyn Idwal in memory of his lost son. According to the legend the lake is haunted by bad omens and no bird of the land will ever fly across it.

The Afanc

Many years ago, a water-dwelling monster plagued the Conwy Valley. This monster, the Afanc, would kill livestock for fun and strike fear into the hearts of the local people. Something had to be done. Hu Gadarn proclaimed he would drag the Afanc away from the Conwy with his strong oxen, and dump it in a deep lake high in the mountains.

First they had to catch the monster, however. The only way to do this was to lure the monster out from under the water using some bait, but what bait should they use? One old woman of the parish had spotted the Afanc's weakness for beautiful young women, so a bold volunteer sat alone on the river bank. As she sang, the Afanc was tempted closer to her, laid its great head upon her lap and was soothed by her gentle song.

The men pounced and threw a large net over the Afanc. They tied and bound it so it could not escape. Using his strong oxen, Hu Gadarn dragged the Afanc up the hill towards Capel Curig and beyond, into the mouth of the Snowdon Horseshoe. The oxen strained hard, one losing an eye as it pulled with all its might. The eye fell out and created the Pool of the Ox's Eye *(Pwll Llygad yr Ych)*. This pool never dries up, despite having no stream or spring to feed it. Eventually they reached Llyn Glaslyn where Hu released the monster and it still swims today.

Beavers

Afanc is the Welsh name for the beaver, which had been hunted to extinction in the UK by the 16th century. It is likely that the name of the legendary beast and Europe's largest rodent arose in parallel from 'river dweller' (after 'afon' – river). In 2009 European beavers were successfully reintroduced to a small area in Scotland and could be re-introduced to Wales as soon as 2011. If the results of an impact study are favourable beavers may once again be seen in the rivers of South West Wales for the first time in nearly 1,000 years (they were last recorded there on the Teifi marshes).

The last battle of King Arthur

King Arthur, long associated with Cornwall, did in fact fight his last battle on the slopes of Snowdon. The site was Bwlch y Saethau on the Watkin Path. His men had taken the ancient fort in Cwm Tregallen and were chasing the enemy up towards the summit of Snowdon. Realising that Arthur's men were catching up with them, the enemy let leash one last rain of arrows as Arthur's men arrived at the top of Bwlch y Saethau. One of these tragically struck Arthur. Arthur was fatally wounded and he asked Bedivere to throw his sword into the lake below (Llyn Glaslyn).

Bedivere set off towards the lake with Arthur's sword, Excalibur, but had second thoughts and decided he would keep the sword as Arthur would surely be dead by now. However, as he returned it became clear that Arthur was hanging on and he knew Bedivere had kept the sword. Bedivere therefore set off once again to fulfil Arthur's wish and toss Excalibur into the deep waters of Llyn Glaslyn. Again, he couldn't bring himself to do it. As he returned Arthur lay dying but not yet departed and once again he instructed Bedivere to throw Excalibur into the lake. Accepting that he had to act honestly, Bedivere returned to the waters where this time he cast the sword high into the air above the lake.

As the sword fell to the water's surface, a hand rose up from the deep to grab it. The hand waved the sword three times then sunk under the water. Arthur's men then carried his body down to the lake where a boat ferried three beautiful maidens dressed in white to the shore. The maidens took Arthur's body and sailed off into the mist on their journey to Avalon. The knights of King Arthur then led their army back up the Gribin ridge from where they traversed into Slanting Gully on the north face of Lliwedd. There, they reside in a hidden cave until the nation needs them to fight once more.

The forming of Twll Du

Legend has it that the black chasm of Twll Du (Black Hole), commonly known as the Devil's Kitchen, was split asunder 2,000 years ago. With the Roman armies advancing on Snowdonia, the local druids retreated to the top of Pen yr Ole Wen (the Hill of the White Light) where they prayed to the Gods for salvation from the invasion. They prayed to the sun and to the moon for three days and three nights. Towards the end of the third day, a bolt of lightning struck the centre of the steep cliff behind Llyn Idwal and split the face of Clogwyn y Geifr into two.

The deep dark slit in the centre, Twll Du, started to produce mist and cloud. Gradually the mist spread out over the whole of the Glyderau and the rest of Snowdonia before enveloping Anglesey as well. The Roman invasion was hampered by poor visibility and they made only small incursions into the lowlands and valleys of Snowdonia. It's said that Twll Du continues to create mist and this is why there is never a cloud-free day on the high tops of the Glyderau.

The name 'The Devil's Kitchen' came much later, coined by sailors from Merseyside journeying down the coast to collect slate from the Bethesda quarries. As they looked up Nant Ffrancon, they could see cloud spilling out from the great cleft in the rocks.

Poetry and madness on Maen Du'r Arddu

Not far below Clogwyn Du'r Arddu and Llyn Du'r Arddu lies a massive boulder, some 5,000 tonnes in weight. It is said that if two people spend the night on top of this rock then one will come down a great poet while the other will have gone mad. Many years ago, two travelling minstrels put this legend to the test. Huw Bellitta and Huwcyn Sion y Canu spent a summer's night atop the great rock. Huwcyn went on to become a successful singer while Huw became a drunk and faded into obscurity.

Y Tylwyth Teg and Llynnau Mymbyr

Long before these lakes became the playground for canoeists from Plas y Brenin (the National Mountain Centre) they were a favourite haunt of Y Tylwyth Teg (Welsh fairies). A woman once left her baby on the lake shore while she went to work during harvest time on the slopes of Moel Siabod. The mischievous Tylwyth Teg swapped her baby for another.

Although the new baby looked the same, it was very sickly, irritable and always crying. The mother soon realised that this was not her child so consulted a wise man from the south. He told her to take a shovel of salt, heat it up and place it near the window of the baby's bedroom. Lo and behold, the trick worked! When the woman returned to the room, the crying, irritable baby was gone and her own child was in the cot sleeping peacefully.

The hidden treasure of Tryfan

Somewhere on the west flank of Tryfan is a cave where Irish settlers hid their gold when they were ousted from the land. They meant to return, but to this day have not been able to. Many years ago a shepherd was searching the west side of Tryfan for a lost lamb when he came across the treasure in a small well-hidden cave. Within, he saw a table covered in gold guarded by a very vicious dog. He ran off to enlist the help of his brother, but could not find the cave again when they returned to face the dog together.

A few years later the cave was discovered by another local lad. Mindful of how his predecessors had failed to relocate the cave, he took out his knife and used it to whittle wood chips from his crook. With the trail of wood chips from the cave he would be able to return with help, to raid the gold. He set off the next day with a group of strong men to gather their reward from the cave. But there were no wood chips to be seen. Y Tylwyth Teg had been out in the night and gathered up all trace of his trail. So the gold waits, lying undisturbed on the flanks of one of our most popular mountains. The legend suggests that a large Billy goat will, one day, lead someone of Irish ancestry to the secret cave and the hoard of treasure. It could be you!

Tryfan.

Twll Du.

Llynnau Mymbyr.

Snowdon Horsehoe from Llynnau Mymbyr.

THE LAST WORD

It is all too easy to see how climbers and hillwalkers are damaging Snowdonia by driving here in cars, parking in unsightly car parks, eroding away the hillsides and removing vegetation from cliffs. Without us, however, the area would be poorer as our activities are part of the human history and economy of the area. Climbers rarely climb on vegetated cliffs and walkers' paths have been managed to the extent that rare plants can grow right up to their edges. We would do well, however, to think carefully about our impact and try to make ourselves seen as a positive influence on the landscape and the economy of the area. How can we do this?

Transport

The area has very good mainline rail links to Bangor and Llandudno Junction and another line follows the coast down to southern Snowdonia. Inside the Park, there are some private railways such as the Ffestiniog and West Highland Railway which make interesting mountain journeys. The area around Snowdon and Ogwen is served by regular Sherpa buses (with routes and timings designed to be useful to hillwalkers). Although none of these services are perfect, they do offer us the opportunity to reduce our environmental impact. They will only improve if we use them and become involved with projects such as the 'Green Key' scheme.

Sherpa bus.

Litter left on Snowdon.

Shop locally

Instead of loading your car up at a supermarket, why not shop in Snowdonia? All the villages have good shops crying out for your business. Good quality locally produced meat is available in butchers across the park.

Litter

I am always gratified about the lack of litter found on the mountains. It seems to be the only place free of this modern scourge. However, occasionally I am disappointed. I recently followed a route at Tremadog which had discarded cigarette stubs on holds all the way up and the empty packet was occupying the top belay!

Apart from the obvious things like plastic and paper wrappers, we should also consider fruit peel to be litter. A banana skin will take up to a year to decompose, orange peel can take five years and apple cores will encourage scavenger species such as the herring gull. Walking from Capel Curig to Crafant with a group recently, we were mobbed by supposedly wild mountain ponies. Some ponies have learnt that they can get food from walkers and this has led to an unfortunate change in their behaviour. In the US, bears that learn this trick are shot!

Littering is a sin and not taking away litter you find should also be considered one. We have to believe that the small amount of litter we find, with the possible exception of the Snowdon Tourist Paths, has been left accidentally and we should look to each other to keep on top of the detritus.

Volunteering

I hope that you may wish to put something back into the area. You can help by educating your friends about what is acceptable behaviour in the mountains, by shopping locally and spending your money in the many cafés and public houses in the area.

If you wish to do more, there are several ways you can volunteer. Contact the Snowdonia National Park Authority for advice or join a National Trust working holiday in the area. The Snowdonia Society also organise volunteer work days throughout the year. BMC Cymru/Wales organises crag clean-ups and tries to ensure climbing and hillwalking is seen in a positive light in the area. Why not attend your local BMC area meeting?

Snowdonia Society

www.snowdonia-society.org.uk; telephone 01690 720287

The National Trust

www.nationaltrust.org.uk; telephone 01492 860123

Snowdonia National Park

www.eryri-npa.co.uk; telephone 01766 770274

Green Key

www.snowdoniagreenkey.co.uk

Snowdonia Active

www.snowdonia-active.com; telephone 01286 685502

BMC Cymru/Wales

E mail bmccymruwales@live.com

Welsh Pronunciation for Beginners

With Welsh spellings, you say what you see. A combination of letters has a particular sound no matter where it appears, unlike English, which has silent letters (write, rite and right) and words which share letters but sound different (the wind blows and you wind your alarm-clock). So once you have grasped the sounds of Welsh you will be able to pronounce any written word you see. It shares many letter sounds with English e.g. A as in ambulance or cat, M as in man and so on, with the exception of:

Dd pronounced Th as in the

F pronounced as V

Ff pronounced as F

Ll similar to Ch in loch

Ph same as English, i.e. F as in physics

R the Welsh enjoy this letter so roll it to your heart's content, if you can

Si as Sh e.g. siop is pronounced shop

U tends to be pronounced as Ee

W is a double U as in blue or cool

Y has several pronunciations: dyn as in dean but with rounder lips, Llyn as in tin and Cymru as in up

Bibliography

Birds of Britain and Europe, Christopher Perrins, Collins 1987, 0-00-219768-5

Birds Britannica, Mark Cocker & Richard Mabey, Chatto and Windus 2005, 0-701 16907-9

Complete British Insects, Michael Chinery, Collins 2005, 0-00-717966-9

Complete British Trees, Paul Sterry, Collins 2007, 10-0-00-721177-5

Complete British Wildlife, Paul Sterry, Collins 1997, 0-00-220071-6

Creaduriaid Asgwrn-Cefn, Cymdeithas Edward Llwyd, 1994, 09522264-0-5

Flowers and Fables, Jocelyne Lawton, Seren 2006, 1-85411-407-7

Geography an Integrated Approach, David Waugh, Nelson 1995, 0-17-444072-3

Grasses, Ferns, Mosses and Lichens, Roger Phillips, Pan 1980, 0-330-25959-8

Hostile Habitats, Jonathan Gregory et al, Scottish Mountaineering Trust 2006, 0-907 521-93-2

Lichens, Frank S. Dobson, Richmond 2005, 0-85546096-2

Mushrooms and Toadstools, Brian Spooner, Collins 1996, 0-00-719150-2

Planhigion Blodeuol, Conwydd a Rhedyn, Eluned Bebb-Jones et al, Cwmdeithas Edward Llwyd, 2003, 0952-22641-3

Rock Trails Snowdonia, Paul Gannon, Pesda Press 2008, 978-1-906095-04-8

Rumours and Oddities from North Wales, Meirion Hughes and Wayne Evans, Carreg Gwalch 1995, 0-86381-337-2

Snowdonia Park Under Pressure, Rob Collister, Pesda Press 2007, 978-1-906095-01-7

Teach Yourself Geology, David Rothery. Hodder Eductaion 2008, 978-0340958797

The Encyclopaedia of Fungi of Britain and Europe, Michael Jordan, Frances Lincoln 2004, 0-7112-2379-3

The High Kingdom, Reader's Digest 1985

The Physical Geography of Landscape, Roy Collard, Unwin Hyman 1988, 0-7135-2734-X

The Plant Life of Snowdonia, Peter Rhind and David Evans, Gomer Press 2001, 1-84323-044-5

Wild Flowers, David McLintock and RSR Fitter, Collins 1973

Wild Flowersof Britain and N. Europe, David Sutton, Kingfisher 1988, 13-978-1-85697-155-3

Wild Flowers and Where to Find Them (Acid Uplands), Laurie Fallows, Frances Lincoln 2004, 0-7112-2028-X

Wild Flowers by Colour, Marjorie Blamey, Domino 1997, 0-7136-7237-4

Recommended websites

www.bbc.co.uk

www.botanicalkeys.co.uk (an excellent aid in the identification of flowers)

www.british-trees.com

www.nicksspiders.com (a real enthusiast's site for the spider lover)

www.pfaf.org (an incredible website packed full of herbalist's information on hundreds of plant species)

www.pyb.co.uk (especially the Enviro diaries)

www.treesforlife.org.uk (excellent location for tree folklore)

www.uklichens.co.uk

www.ukmoths.org.uk

www.uksafari.com (excellent for beetles and spiders)

www.whatsthiscaterpillar.co.uk (very comprehensive and clear)

www.wikipedia.org

INDEX